RAISING THE SURFACE

WITH MACHINE EMBROIDERY

RAISING THE SURFACE
WITH MACHINE EMBROIDERY

MAGGIE GREY

BATSFORD

Introduction

I have always found that textured surfaces hold a deep fascination for me. Gnarled old tree trunks, crumbling carved walls, cliff faces, and old worn artefacts – these excite me and move me towards the act of creating embroideries. This obsession has quite literally grown out from the fabric and become truly three-dimensional. Items such as cuffs, bowls, vessels, and towers have been the subject of recent work. This book aims to explore the possibilities of raising the surface of embroidery, starting with stitch as texture and working through to three-dimensional pieces.

The book begins with a chapter on backgrounds and suggests some possible starting points for the journey. It proceeds through ideas for working on these surfaces to produce low-relief embroidery with the use of textural stitches. In subsequent chapters, the surface is raised by means of a variety of techniques and media. From everyday items such as straws and chopsticks to the use of artists' texturing media and exciting products such as paper modelling paste, polymer clays, and heat-moulding foam, all avenues are explored. Most of the products used are easily obtainable, usually from art suppliers.

A section on frames offers the chance to move away from the purchase of commercial frames to introduce a finish that complements the whole work. The final chapter is devoted to three-dimensional shape and form.

Although new materials are introduced, at no stage is the use of stitch neglected. Sometimes it is understated and used as a means of underpinning a construction, sometimes exaggerated using heavy thread or string beneath a surface, but it is always there. In this book some hand embroidery is used with the free machine techniques to complement or add texture. A swing-needle sewing machine with the ability to drop the feed-dogs is all that is needed.

Sources of inspiration are considered. In addition to the natural world there are all sorts of wonderful artefacts in museums. Archaeological books, too, are an excellent treasure trove – look out for peeling paint and rust.

The ideas detailed in this book should be considered a starting point for your own experiments with raised embroidery.

Fossil Layers (65 x 32 cm/25^1/$_2$ x 12^1/$_2$ in; detail). An embroidery based on a study of fossils. Painted and gilded Model Magic modelling paste was used as a base. Hand and machine embroidery integrated the fossils with the background.

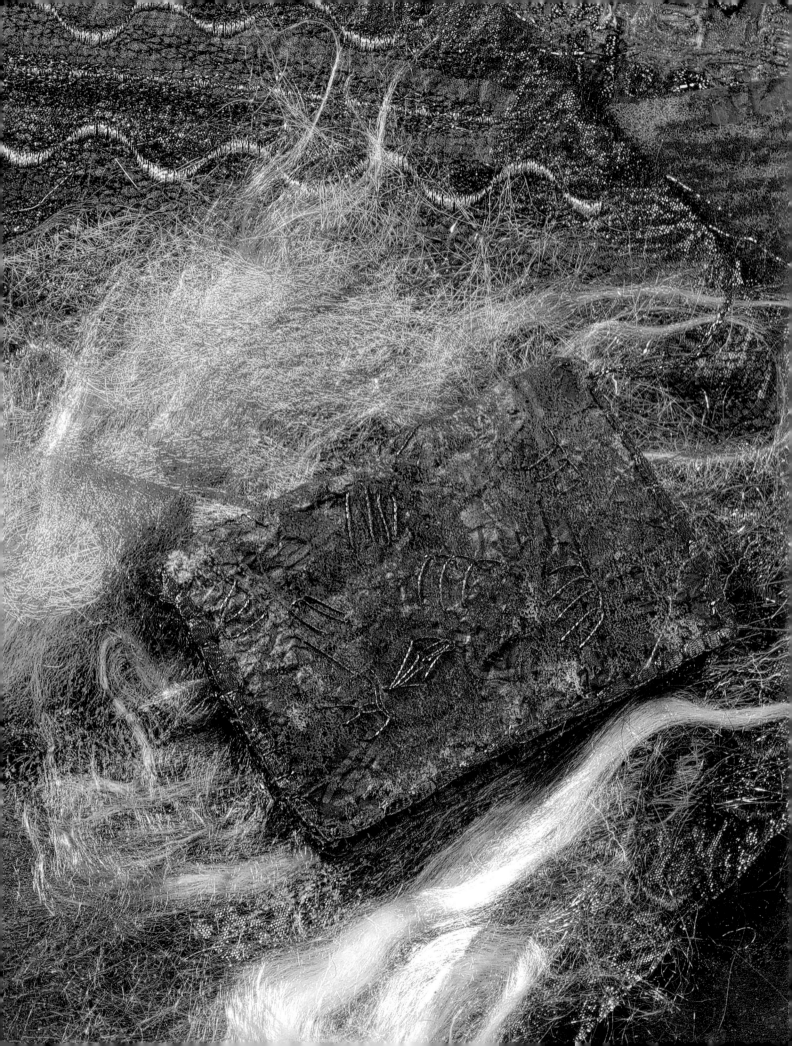

Chapter 1

Making Backgrounds

Before beginning to build texture into a low-relief surface, it is a good idea to make a base fabric to use as a background. You may have a favourite fabric decoration technique that would be suitable but, if not, here are a few of my favourites to start you off.

Materials

In this chapter we will use the following:

- Angelina fibres in two or three colours. These do not look very promising at first glance. Resembling plastic-like strands of tinsel, they are transformed when gently heated with an iron to allow them to bond together and change colour in a most delightful way. They need to be used in a considered manner with other fabrics, and ways of doing this are demonstrated below, where they are used to build up exciting backgrounds.

- Fine chiffon, together with iron-on foils, which can be heat-treated for a crunchy textured surface.

- Brown paper – ordinary brown paper, as sold in stationers' shops – which becomes something unique when combined with painted Bondaweb (fusible webbing).

- A variety of fabric scraps that will be transformed into a richly stitched embroidery.

- Special papers to transfer computer designs to fabric.

Background 1: Angelina fibres

To make a fabric, lay a mixture of different-coloured Angelina fibres on non-stick parchment paper, cover with more paper and press lightly with an iron on the silk setting. You will have a delightful, gauzy, glittery piece of fabric that you can lay over a base fabric (dark shows off the colour best) for further stitching.

This is the basis for using these fibres. However, they are very shiny and need knocking back if they are to be successfully integrated into your work. This can be done in a variety of ways.

Silk-painted Bondaweb (fusible webbing) is pressed onto a piece of chiffon. Make sure that you paint the rough side of the webbing and allow to dry thoroughly. Angelina is then laid on top and more chiffon placed on top of this (remember to place parchment paper over your ironing surface first). The resulting fabric is then 'zapped' very lightly on the Bondaweb (fusible webbing) side with a heat tool to expose some of the Angelina.

Press Bondaweb (fusible webbing) onto some dark velvet (the cheap, stretchy sort is fine). Place a thin layer of Angelina fibres on the Bondaweb (fusible webbing) and press with the iron at the silk setting. This can be varied in a number of ways, for example:

Angelina and viscose tops bonded using Supermend powder.

- Try painting the Bondaweb (fusible webbing) first. Add a little Angelina and press. You could also add some silk or nylon tops (the carded fibres). These are good because they provide a contrast against the Angelina and take off some of the shine. A little of them goes a long way.

- Try using a Markal (Shiva) oilstick on the Bondaweb (fusible webbing) and spreading the Angelina in some areas only.

- Use a contrasting Angelina in a grid pattern. Lay down fibres of one colour first and then add the contrasting colour in a pattern over the top. Press carefully.

- The Angelina can be used directly on net if a little Supermend (bonding powder) is applied to the net before the fibres are placed over it. Again, remember to cover the ironing surface with parchment paper. On the net side, this has a distinctly reptilian look.

- Bonding powder can also be used with silk tops and Angelina. Just arrange a mix of silk or viscose and the fibres on the parchment paper. Sprinkle with powder and press it as before. This makes a very delicate 'floaty' fabric that will probably need some sort of backing before it can be stitched.

Any of the above pieces could be stitched by hand, or free-machined to be used as a background. Motifs can be applied and more Angelina, as a film, could be placed over the motifs and stitched down. Sheer fabric, or net, can be used in places over the Angelina to knock back the shine. You could also

Cross Purposes (12 x 20 cm/4³/₄ x 8 in). Angelina fibres, heated and applied to velvet with overlays of net and sheer fabrics. Motifs were formed from lines of satin stitch on felt, cut out and machined to the base with free running stitch. Further Angelina was applied over part of the motifs.

just use cold-water-dissolvable fabric over the pure Angelina film. Stitch by hand or machine and then dissolve away the backing. A method is given in Chapter 3 to combine this yarn with other threads and use a heat-reactive thread to distort it.

Background 2: Fine chiffon sandwich

The chiffon sandwich is a useful device. Make a sandwich using two pieces of very sheer chiffon or scarves, foil and Bondaweb (fusible webbing). To do this place some parchment paper on the ironing surface and lay one of the chiffon pieces on top. Then press on the Bondaweb (fusible webbing). While it is still warm from the iron, place some foil on it, shiny side up. Rub with your thumbnail or a blunt knife-edge or spoon to transfer the foil to the webbing. Don't cover too thickly. If it gets cold and stops transferring, just switch the iron to the silk setting and rub the toe of the iron over the foil to transfer it. The Bondaweb (fusible webbing) should be well covered. Pull away the clear top sheet of the foil. When you have sufficient colour on the Bondaweb (fusible webbing), press the other piece of chiffon over the top. Use parchment paper to protect the iron.

The warm sandwich can now be laid over a background such as velvet and pressed down firmly. It can then be zapped with a heat gun – lightly or heavily, depending on the effect you want to produce. It will result in a textured, lacy fabric that clings to the velvet below it – lovely with space-dyed velvet. If necessary, cover with parchment paper and press **very lightly** to ensure adhesion to the base fabric. Many fabrics can be used instead of the velvet. Experiment:

- Try adding some slivers of Angelina fibres to the sandwich and zap very lightly to avoid discolouring the Angelina.

Bondaweb (fusible webbing) is ironed onto the first piece of chiffon and metallic foil is placed, shiny side up, on top. This is ironed to the Bondaweb and the second piece of chiffon is ironed over the top.

- If you wish, you could add more detail by stitching on the velvet or base fabric before placing the chiffon sandwich on top. A linear design of built-in sewing machine patterns would work really well.

- The chiffon sandwich could be backed with water-soluble fabric, placed in a frame and free-machined. Wash away the backing and dry well before zapping. Apply to a prepared backing using further stitching rather than melting onto the velvet.

Chiffon sandwiches can also be used to recover a disaster – just lay the sandwich on top of the piece that has gone wrong and zap. You can also try zapping the sandwich on its own and then tearing it into delicate, distressed pieces that can be applied to any piece of work to add depth.

Layers of fine chiffon were sandwiched together using Bondaweb (fusible webbing) and iron-on foil. The results were placed over velvets or painted fabrics and a heat tool was used to distress and fuse the chiffon to the background fabric. The piece on the far left shows a sandwich 'zapped' over heavy machine embroidery.

Background 3:
Brown paper and Bondaweb (fusible webbing)

Painted Bondaweb (fusible webbing), pressed onto crumpled, painted brown paper, gives a remarkable effect. Try the following:

- Cut the Bondaweb (fusible webbing) so that it is slightly smaller than the paper.

- Paint the Bondaweb (fusible webbing) with silk paints on the textured side.

- Paint the brown paper with any medium – silk paints, acrylics, coloured inks, etc.

- Allow both to dry and then gently crumple the brown paper until it becomes soft and rag-like.

- Bond the brown paper onto a backing fabric such as cotton, calico, or felt using Bondaweb (fusible webbing) on the backing fabric, not the brown paper. Peel off the backing paper and press down the brown paper. Don't press too hard or the crinkles will be ironed out. Press lightly to help it to stick.

- Very carefully, press the painted Bondaweb (fusible webbing) onto the brown paper. Again, don't press too hard – just light pressure and the heat of the iron (on the cotton setting) will transfer the painted webbing. Do not iron for too long.

- Peel off the backing paper when it is cool, holding down the webbing where it has a tendency to lift.

When completely cold, use metallic wax very lightly to highlight the filigree effect of the Bondaweb

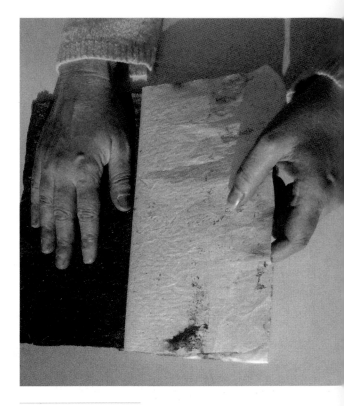

Painted Bondaweb (fusible webbing) is peeled away from the brown paper.

(fusible webbing). Stampers' embossing powder can be used instead. If you scatter a little over the work while the webbing is still warm from the iron, it will stick and can be heated with a heat tool. Don't heat for too long or it will zap the webbing too.

The effect varies according to whether thick or thin brown paper is used. Both give good results. You may find that this technique needs a little practice; the temperature of the iron is crucial. Once mastered, it can produce delightful results and, because the paper is bonded to fabric, it is a strong and resilient base. Further variations could involve computer printing the brown paper first, or painting a defined pattern onto it before crumpling.

Red Hot Earth (25 x 25 cm/10 x 10 in). Fossil shapes, quilted into painted silk, form
the centre of this fossil study. Brown paper and painted Bondaweb (fusible webbing)
on a felt backing was burned into shapes with a soldering iron and applied
in layers around the silk.around the silk.

Background 4: Strippy backgrounds

I call these strippy backgrounds because you start with strips or pieces of fabric on a background, cover with sheers and then use lots of machine stitching to bring it all together. Colours need to be considered very carefully, as too much contrast or too glitzy a strip will stand out and take an awful lot of stitching.

To achieve this result, take a firm base of cotton or calico. Place a further fabric on this, one that tones with all the cut strips. A spray of temporary fabric adhesive such as 505 Spray is very useful here. Then cut or tear the small pieces that are going on top of this, using 505 Spray to hold them down. Put a layer of sheer fabric (chiffon, net, or a mixture of the two) on top in places.

Now a lot of stitching is needed. This can be done with the normal foot in place and the feed-dogs up. Use a zigzag or fairly open pattern stitch initially, and build up the stitches using toning threads. When the pieces are well blended, add some heavier pattern stitching, or free-machine using satin-stitch blobs – bursts of satin stitch here and there. Colourwashed effects can be achieved if the pieces are chosen carefully, or the colours could change from one colour at the top to another at the bottom, with a mixture of the fabrics in the centre.

Above: Fragments and strips of fabric are laid over a background. A temporary adhesive is helpful to keep them in place while they are stitched with massed pattern or zigzags.
Right: *Inch Strand Beach* by Barbara Taylor. This large bolster cushion was inspired by the colours of the beach in Dingle, Ireland. Strips of fabric were laid on a neutral background and lots of stitching was worked over the top to merge the colours. Barbara's working sample is shown.

Making Backgrounds 17

Background 5: Computer print

Many people have access to a personal computer and a paint or draw program. These can be used to make exciting designs that can then be transferred to fabric in several ways. If you are planning a fabric for a background, don't make the design too complicated. Just use some of the tools to splatter colour over a solid ground. Alternatively, using one of the built-in textures can provide an excellent base for further work. The diagram (right) shows some more ideas.

Of course, if you are planning particular motifs, such as fossils, flowers, or leaves, you could scan a picture or drawing, or use a digital photograph. Make your design based on that, and use it as a base for further stitching. Use some of the special effects to simplify shapes so that it is not too busy.

The design could be transferred to fabric using one of the following methods:

- T-shirt transfer paper, available from large stationers or computer supply shops. Look for the cool-peel packs as they peel off more easily. This method can make the fabric a little stiff, which is good for free-machining. Press under parchment paper with a hot iron to remove the waxiness.

- Soak the fabric in a special solution, such as Bubble Jet Set, before printing directly onto the fabric. Instructions for this are provided on the bottle.

- Use a transfer film such as Lazertran which can put your image onto anything from fabric to clay.

- Try special fabric which is ready to put through your printer. This is expensive but gives really good results.

So now you have a starting point for this exploration of raised texture in embroidery.

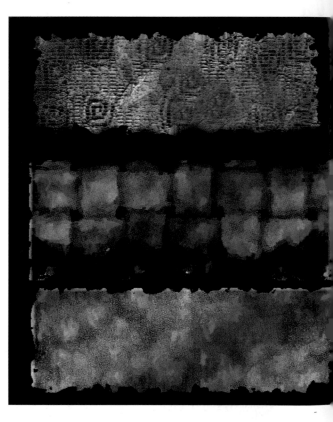

Computer designs: *Top* the paint brush tool is used to make a base. This is textured with a special effect and overprinted with a brush shape. *Centre* Paint brush tool as before with smudged swirls. The Weave effect is then applied. *Below* Letters are used as a paper texture with pastel colours and a chalk effect.

Halina Davies used a design source of medieval floor tiles for this work (26 x 40 cm/10$^1/_4$ x 15$^3/_4$ in). She scanned her photographs into a paint program and used a special effect called 'Brush Strokes' to simplify the design. This was transferred to calico and the tile designs were stitched onto it. The soft background is hand-made silk paper with the same design printed onto it.

Margaret Talbot designed and made this colourful embroidery (21 x 29 cm/8$^1/_4$ x 11$^1/_2$ in) by layering different fabrics, all created by ironing on T-shirt transfer paper. The base was nylon and the upper layers a 'stitch-and-tear' material. These upper layers were cut out with a soldering iron. Gold paint was used on the edges and the entire piece placed on felt and machine stitched to give a lightly quilted effect.

Chapter 2

Raising the Surface a Little

Having decided on a background, it is time to consider using stitch, both hand and machine, to raise the surface and add texture and form.

Materials and equipment

In addition to a variety of threads and yarns of different weight and strips of torn fabric, we will use knitting ribbons, which are tubular knitted yarns that can be purchased in some lovely colours or in natural shades for dyeing. These are also available in net, to add further interesting possibilities. Try knitting-wool shops for these and other interesting yarns.

Water-soluble paper is sold as an alternative to water-soluble fabric. I don't find it robust enough in general for this purpose, but when used with a resist it is great. It can take quite heavy stitching before the resist is applied and the remainder washed away using cold water. An enormous variety of textures can be created using this material and it will take paint and speciality waxes and finishes very well. It also combines well with Puff Paint, which we will use throughout this book.

Rubber stamps and the Flower Stitcher foot.

Acrylic felt is also used, in particular the type that reacts to a heat tool. The advent of embossing enamels, easily available from stampers' supply shops, adds lots of new ideas for the embroiderer, especially when combined with stitch.

In this chapter the Flower Stitcher is introduced. This is a special foot that fits a variety of machines. It stitches circles of various sizes, and can be used to create some exciting effects. It is not too expensive and is a useful addition to the range of built-in machine stitches.

Do think about using a design source. There are lots of possibilities for textural inspiration, especially in the natural world. Look at trees, plants, seed-heads, stones. Take photographs, cut out magazine illustrations, do some rough sketches, crumple up papers and stick them down. Collect all these together to make an 'ideas book'. It can be a very scruffy affair – nobody needs to see it but you. You will find it wonderfully useful for future projects.

An ideas book can contain drawings, rough paintings or small samples of stitch. It is very useful as an *aide-memoire* for both inspiration and application. (MG)

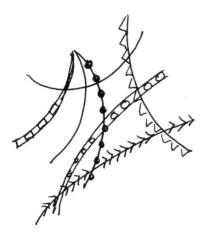

Curved lines,
mixed and straight pattern

Curved lines,
parallel mixed patterns

Stitched loops,
mixed patterns

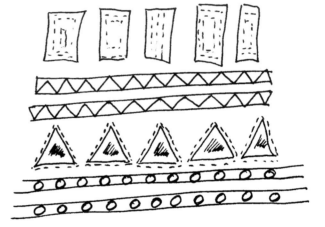

Shapes – straight stitch outlines with inner patterns
(Consider the shapes in between – the negative shapes)

Geometric shapes with bands between,
straight lines and mixed patterns

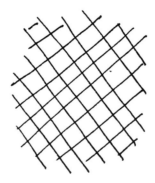

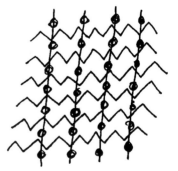

Random grid

Regular grid – straight stitch

Regular grid – pattern

Stitch direction

Even if you don't go as far as the ideas book, try to plan your lines of stitching when experimenting with some of the following techniques. The diagrams, left, shows some possible starting points. This will always be better than random wavy lines stitched as the fancy takes you.

Machining into raised strips

A variety of techniques can be used to add texture using raised strips or cords. It usually helps to couch down the threads by hand and then to free-machine into them. Try knotting a bunch of threads together and then stitching into them using free running stitch so that the knots stand proud of the machining.

You could try your hand at a crocheted cord. Just a simple chain, as shown here, can be very useful. Start by tying the yarn around the hook. Then just draw the thread through the tied yarn. Continue like this to make a long chain. Cut the yarn and pull it through to finish off.

Crochet several different types of yarn together to obtain either a contrast or a harmonious look. When several chains have been completed, place them on a background ready to be machine embroidered. A simple painted silk background provides an excellent contrast for the chunky crochet chains. Alternatively, a chiffon sandwich gives a great surface for them to nestle into. The machine stitching can be light to show the crochet effect, or heavy to bed the chain into the background. To emphasize the texture, stitch right into the plait at the edges and run some of the stitching across the chain too. I find that a thread slightly darker than the background works well for bedding-in the crochet.

Making crochet chain.

Above: Crochet chains were laid over a zapped chiffon sandwich. Further free-machine stitching was then worked over the top of the chains. This makes a good base for further stitching or could be used for cushions or book covers.

Right: A part-stitched sample showing knitting ribbons stuffed with wool. Stitching into the ribbons makes them part of the painted background. This was achieved with free running stitch worked into the edges and over the ribbons to form bumps.

The technique of using thick wool or thread to stuff tubular knitting ribbons is not new and, when stuffed, these have a variety of uses. However, they gain a new lease of life when they are couched to a background and then heavily machine embroidered. Use a bodkin or darning needle and thick wool to stuff them. Then tack by hand to the background in swirls or shapes. Plan the design beforehand for best results. Free-machine using either a toning or contrasting colour, allowing the knitting ribbon to show as silky bumps. Consider the thread that you are using for the free running stitch: if the knitting ribbons are silky, use a cotton-based thread to stitch into them. Some are available in lovely colourways. This will provide a good contrast. Different effects can be obtained using this method according to whether you stitch around the edges and 'nibble' into the ribbon or stitch heavily over it.

Another way to use stuffed knitting ribbons is to couch them to a painted fabric, perhaps adding some extra hand stitching and beads. Then make a 'chiffon sandwich' as described in Chapter 1. Lay this over the top and work a little free running stitch (avoiding the beads) to hold it down. Zap with a heat tool and the chiffon will disintegrate over the textured surface.

It is possible to obtain tubular stitched 'ribbons' made from brightly coloured net. An alternative is to make rouleaux of net – little stitched tubes made by folding a 1.25 cm (¹/₂ in) strip of net in half and stitching along the long edge. This is then either turned inside out or simply cut close to the seam and stuffed. The net could be lightly machined with an open pattern before the tube is made. The material used to stuff the ribbons will show far more and could include beads. The net rouleaux are difficult to stuff using the darning-needle method so I usually cut a short length of firm plastic straw and thread the stuffing thread through that. The results can be used in the same way as the stuffed ribbons described earlier or can be incorporated into the plaits used in the next section.

Plaits

Plaited strips of fabric or thread can be used to raise the surface and add texture. The plaits could be made from the same yarns in different colourways, or from a mixture of yarns. These all give different effects and the ends will form tassels when they are tied. The resultant plait can be stitched down by hand, perhaps using a decorative stitch to attach it. For example, the horizontal bars of raised chain band could be used to hold down the plait and the actual chain stitch could then be worked across it. The plaits could be stitched by machine, as described for the crochet chains.

In addition to plaited threads, it is possible to achieve a good surface by tearing painted or dyed fabrics, such as silk, and treating them in the same way. My own favourite trick is to dye kitchen cloths – the ones with little holes in them – rip them into 1.25 cm (¹/₂ in) strips and then plait them with ribbons or shiny fabrics. The torn ends make great tassels. Machining into these strips can also give an exciting finish to a piece of work. Extend the idea of the plait by using unusual materials and/or wires in it. The 'zappable' acrylic felt that disintegrates with heat could be cut into strips and each strip stitched with a pattern or free-machined. Then a heat tool can be used on the strips to distress them and produce textured strips for plaiting.

Plait these strips with some of the stuffed knitting ribbons or crocheted chains to create some highly unusual bands. Strips of net stitched with heavy machining in metallic threads, with the edges torn, make another good addition. A further possibility for inclusion is a pipe-cleaner threaded with beads at regular intervals – being stiff, this can add structure to a plait. Thread the beads on first and manipulate them into place as you plait, bending them into a curve or forming a sharp angle, as shown in the diagram, right.

Top: Dyed kitchen wipes (J-cloths) are torn into strips, plaited with ribbons and stitched to a background. The ends are unplaited to form tassels. (MG)
Above: Pipe-cleaners and beads plaited with yarns and ribbons. Bend the pipe-cleaner so the bead is on the angle.

Right: Wrapped pipe-cleaners and beads were combined with net strips, cut 'zapped' felt and other yarns to produce plaits. These could be joined together to form a fabric or could be used as edgings for a panel. Three or four plaits would make a good cover for a book.

Below: *Elizabethan Cuff.* Plaits were hand-stitched together to form a cuff. The pipe-cleaners were bent into regular shapes with beads at the angle. This formed a regular pattern when the strips were joined. Large bugle beads were used on the pipe-cleaners forming the lower edge.

It is possible to get pipe-cleaners in black, gold, or bright colours in craft or toy shops. They are even better when wrapped with thread. This could be done by hand, which is surprisingly quick if a thick yarn is used, and 'bumps' can be made by winding more thickly in places. Alternatively, use a sewing machine set on a wide zigzag with the feed-dogs dropped. Pass the pipe-cleaner through slowly to cover well or quickly to show the colour below.

The bands produced by this method could be joined by hand or machine embroidery to produce an entire fabric suitable for bags or book covers. The pipe-cleaners allow shapes to be made and held and are suitable for three-dimensional work.

Cable stitch

This stitch uses the bobbin as the main thread. Winding a heavier thread onto the bobbin and by-passing the bobbin tension can result in a glorious mass of texture. The work can then be turned upside down, so that the bubbly threads are on top, and free running stitch (using normal top and bottom threads) can be worked over the top. Alternatively, it can be an interesting exercise to work some of the decorative stitches that are built into your sewing machine over the top.

Net is a wonderful material to use with cable stitch as it is a halfway house between water-soluble fabric and sheers. It slightly distorts stitching and can be torn easily. Try to find the stiff net, sometimes called ballet net, and use it double. It will probably be necessary to frame the net (very carefully, as it tears easily – use a spring frame). I like to machine embroider on net using a fairly narrow zigzag. The holes in the net force the stitch into interesting shapes. If you use this stitch for outlines and then fill with cable stitch in free running you will get a good result. A good mixture of threads is called for and metallics add their own special gleam. Experiment to find out the best way of using metallic threads both on the top and in the bobbin. Machines vary in the way they handle threads for cable stitching.

A design (20 x 25 cm/ 8 x 10 in) was stitched on net using a zigzag stitch. Areas of the design were worked upside down using a heavy thread in the bobbin to give added emphasis.

Red Cross (26 x 17 cm/
10^1/$_4$ x 6^3/$_4$ in) – a cruciform
piece with a background of
strippy fabrics and heavy
stitching. The cross was
'zapped' acrylic felt with
applied flower-stitched
circles on water-soluble fabric. Buttonholed rings provide a change of scale. The
water-soluble fabric strip
shows the underlying grid.

With the Flower Stitcher, a variety of effects is possible using different stitches, and this can be very useful if you have a limited range of pattern stitches on your machine. This foot fits most machines, but do check that yours is suitable before buying the foot. You may need an extension shank for your machine to use the foot, and bear in mind that it may need oiling before you use it.

Used with a heavier bobbin thread, it provides a well-defined shape that can be stitched on felt, cut out and applied to a background, bobbin-stitched side up, by free-machine stitching into the shape. This works well on water-soluble fabric, too – as you can see from the book cover shown on page 60. I have also stitched beads onto the cut-out rings and painted both the beads and the stitching with acrylic paints before applying them to the background. For a stronger effect, dab the cut-out circle with a Puff Paint such as Xpandaprint. Heat with a heat tool and paint using acrylics before applying.

Zapping felt for texture

Many acrylic felts can be heated with a heat tool to form a heavily textured surface. Not all felts do this but those sold as 'Kunin' felt are more likely to work. Do test for 'zappability' before stitching, and remember to wear a mask or respirator and to work in a very well-ventilated room.

To use to maximum effect for texture, try stitching strips of felt, by hand, machine, or a mixture of both. Zap with a heat tool and the felt will disintegrate to leave the stitching with a textured border. Apply these strips to the background, considering the placement of the strips to give a strong design. As an alternative to this, the felt strips could be cut out and stitched to a background before zapping, but you will need to consider the effect of the heat tool on the prepared background.

This material works particularly well when combined with a fabric that does not respond so quickly to heat. Silk, in particular, is a good choice. Try stitching squares of painted silk onto the felt in a grid (see right).

The edges of the squares could be satin stitched, burnt with a candle or they could be torn. A little light machine embroidery could be worked between the squares, or a very open pattern stitch could be used. When the piece is zapped with a heat tool, the felt will become distressed but the silk will remain untouched.

This basic technique could be expanded. For example, the silk could be applied to the background using standard appliqué techniques. Try cut-back appliqué, where the silk is laid over the felt, having been sprayed with a temporary adhesive like 505 Spray to hold it. An outline design

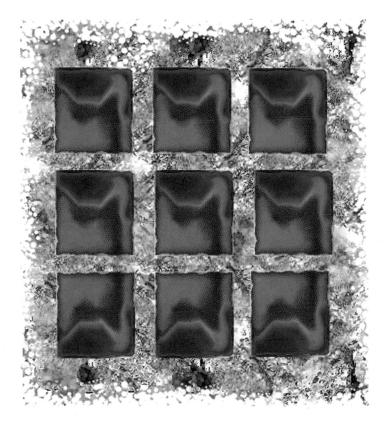

Squares of silk placed
on heat-reactive felt.

Susan Stuart named her piece *'A relic of something-that-might-have-been'* (16 x 20 cm/6^1/$_4$ x 8 in). Dyed silk squares, under metallic and polyester sheer fabrics, were embellished with metallic thread stitches. The whole piece was then zapped with a heat gun, placed on cotton velvet and lightly padded to stabilize the fragile areas.

is then stitched in free running stitch on the silk. Finally the silk is cut to the stitching, and a narrow line of satin stitch (about 3 mm/⅛ in) is stitched to cover the edge. Several lines of free running stitch around the edge would also work well and could give a lighter effect than the satin stitch. Further free-machining can be used to add details. I find that this technique works really well for 'tiled' pieces, where the silk is applied to the felt and then the felt is cut out as a square. This can then be applied over a rich background like strippy fabrics, before zapping. Just a few hand stitches can be used to apply the tiles so that they sit loosely on the top, giving a raised effect.

Alternatively, place the tiles on two layers of net before stitching and fix them to the net with stitch before zapping.

Another twist to this technique is to apply the silk, as before, but use a slightly larger shape and stitch several lines following the shape – as shown in the diagram below. Then, when complete, zap the back first to remove the felt from behind the motif. Turn over and zap as before. The applied area will crinkle and look quilted.

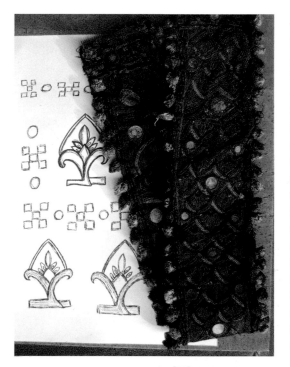

Left: A Sind (Pakistan) money belt is used as inspiration. Motifs from the belt are drawn and used in a felt sample. (MG)
Below: Tiles on net. A heat gun was used to distort the acrylic felt. Motifs drawn on silk were stitched to the felt, following the main lines of the shape. The excess silk was cut away and the entire piece was treated by the heat tool. The felt distorts but the silk does not. The small sample shows the same technique with lines of stitch on the motif.

Lines of stitch around a motif.

Pethia (Children) by Alice Kettle (16 x 16 cm/6^1/$_4$ x 6^1/$_4$ in).
Heavy machine embroidery produced contours in the
fabric. This gives this small study its shape and liveliness.

Heavy machine stitching

Free-machining, worked densely, can be used to
shape a piece of work or the item could be hand
stitched to raise the surface.

Try working very heavy stitching and using
changes of direction to manipulate the shape. To
add weight, use two threads in the needle or
consider putting a heavier thread in the bobbin
(cable stitch) and working from the back of the
piece. Heavy circular stitching can raise the centre
of a circle, for instance. Curved sweeps and spirals
are also good for contorted stitching. Make a
sampler trying out this technique and keep it as a
note of the effects obtained.

A great deal of distortion was achieved in the
'Ancient Faces' piece (right) in which very heavy
stitching enabled the face to be manipulated into
shape. Hand stitching was then worked into this. It
was deliberately used lightly to blend with the
machine stitching; open stitches, such as fly stitch,
work best here. Sometimes it is hard to get
definition when thick layers of machining are used,
and the hand stitching can add this focus.

Ancient Faces (60 x 36 cm/23¹/₂ x 14 in). Based on Roman grave portraits, this work used a base of felt so that the sections could be cut out and pieced together. The stitching was very heavy and stitch direction was used to form contours. Felt gives good results with this technique as it distorts well.

Another felt example. This small bag, with a Chinese flavour, was made from heavily machined strips of felt with additional hand stitching. The strips were cut out and rejoined, making use of the shaped edges. The large tassel and small 'danglies' were also made from stitched felt shapes. The smaller embellishments were rectangles of stitching, rolled and caught down with a hand stitch.

It can be useful to work in bands, maybe using cable stitch as a starting point and then turning the work over and stitching into it with free running stitch. Remember to turn the piece over when working the cable stitch. I usually stitch on felt as it can be cut without fraying and distorts well, if this is required. The bands of heavy stitching can be cut out and woven or could be joined using insertion stitches. Some shaped bands could be worked to form a contrast to the straight lines. Hand stitches such as chain, raised chain band, and running stitch may be worked over the top of the machine stitching to add definition. Use a sharp needle and stitch into the top layer of the threads only. The work is usually too heavy to pull a needle right through to the back.

Water-soluble paper

This is a special paper that can be stitched and then washed away in much the same way as a dissolvable fabric. It is not as robust as the usual water-soluble fabrics, so is not so good for normal stitching. Its great advantage is in its ability to take a resist, which will prevent all of the paper from being washed away. When considering texture, a very important plus for this paper is the effect achieved when the dissolvable paper is used with Puff Paint and is then layered. Try the following method:

1   Use the paper double and stitch in a random fashion with a fairly open zigzag stitch. The stitching may not show very much in the finished piece but it is absolutely crucial as it forms an infrastructure that holds everything together. The stitching can be in straight lines or can weave around in curves.

2   Make two or three pieces in this way, depending on how raised a texture you need. The top piece should not be as heavily stitched as the others, to allow more holes. This piece could also have some patterns worked on it if your sewing machine can cope with the paper. Note that satin stitch patterns sometimes cause the paper to tear.

3   When the stitching is complete, dab with a sponge dipped in Puff Paint. Use it sparingly – don't apply too much. Heat with a heat gun when the Puff Paint is dry. Hold the gun high so as not to singe the paper.

Liberty bodice. Detail from a bodice made from strips of water-soluble paper, heat-moulding foam and vanishing muslin.

4   Now it is time to paint on the resist. This could be a gel medium like Pebeo Gel (available in glass shops for glass painting), nail varnish, or even acrylic paint. Paint it over the stitching and over any areas that you want to resist. Although it is not essential to work a stitched grid as on cold-water-soluble fabric, you should make sure that all sections are joined using the resist – otherwise an isolated section could float away. Be more sparing with the resist on the top piece as you need more holes here. Don't be too heavy handed with the resist or you will get pieces that are too chunky: think lacy.

5   Pin the pieces (one at a time) on a polystyrene tile (or similar). Fill a bowl with water and use a paintbrush to apply the water to the water-soluble paper. Keep applying water with the brush until the paper starts to wash away. The paper will be very 'sludgy' and you can use your fingers to make holes in it and then push the pulp onto adjacent areas to make heavier deposits. Dab gently with kitchen paper to remove some of the water. Then put it in a warm place to dry, which will take some time. Repeat the process with the other layers.

6   When the pieces are all dry, paint them with acrylic paint. You will get a better feeling of depth if you make the lower layer a little darker. Use two or three colours to vary the surface. Allow the paint to dry.

7   When dry, place the lower layer on a backing fabric to give it more stability. This can be felt or calico, if it is not to show, or a painted fabric. Place the other layers on top – do move the layers around and try different combinations to get the best effect. Stitch all the layers together by hand using a stab stitch (up from the bottom and straight down again) and finish with a little metallic wax or a dry brush of gold paint to enhance the surface. You can also dab with embossing ink and sprinkle with embossing powder, which will give a very textured metallic effect when heated and will strengthen the piece.

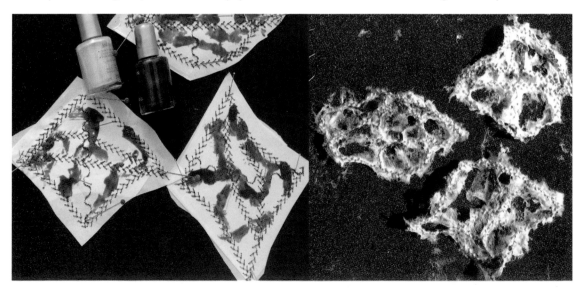

Left: Water-soluble paper is lightly stitched and a resist is then applied.
Right: After washing away the unwanted paper, the pieces are dried ready for painting. (MG)

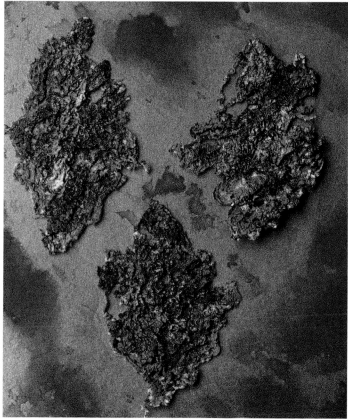

Above: After painting, the pieces are ready for gilding and layering using hand-stitching techniques. (MG)
Right: Metallic tiles made by layering pieces of water-soluble paper, painted to give a metallic effect. They give the appearance of rusting, degraded metals. (MG)

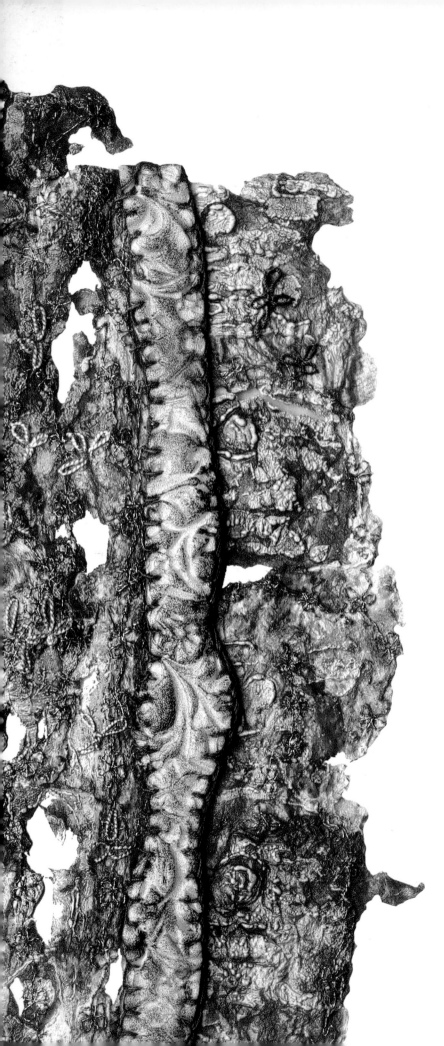

Stitching water-soluble paper directly onto fabric

It is possible to stitch the first layer of water-soluble paper straight onto a backing fabric. Try it on a dark felt, for instance. Follow the directions for stitching and resisting and then pin the whole thing on a polystyrene tile to dissolve it. Push the excess paper with your finger, as before, but push it onto an unpapered area of the backing fabric. Dry and paint, as before, adding other colours as required. Coloured metallic waxes, applied lightly with your finger, give the finishing touch.

Left: Sample for Liberty bodice. This used water-soluble paper with Puff Paint, which gave a delicious fragility when the paper was dissolved.

Opposite: Sample by Monica Morgan using a foam stamp with an Art Nouveau look. This was used to print Puff Paint onto water-soluble paper. After stitching, the paint was heated and some of the paper washed away. Painting with acrylics produced a lovely piece waiting to be applied to a background with further stitch.

Stamping water-soluble paper with Puff Paint

A very interesting texture can be obtained by stamping water-soluble paper with Puff Paint and a rubber stamp or wooden block. A simple stamp gives the best effect. I prefer the Xpandaprint brand as it gives a more raised effect. It is possible to obtain exciting results in this way, which can range from very heavy and textural effects to a light, cobweb-like material. Make some samples to check the results before you make a big piece, and work to a plan or design if possible.

Method

Use water-soluble paper as a single sheet. Spoon a little Puff Paint onto a sheet of glass, perspex, or heavy plastic and mix a tiny amount of coloured acrylic paint into it. If you use too much it will not puff. The idea is just to see where the stamp is when you stitch. Brush or roll it to an even consistency – not too thick. Use a rubber stamp or wooden block (wash the paint from this and any brushes as soon as you can; don't let it dry) and place it face down into the Puff Paint and then print on the water-soluble paper. Make a little pad of kitchen towel to put under the paper and it will print better. Continue to print, adding more Puff Paint as necessary until all the areas in your design have been printed. Allow to dry naturally. Now do a little stitching, following the lines of the block. This helps to hold the piece together. Then puff the paint using a heat tool or an iron. Don't keep the heat tool in one place for too long or it will scorch the paper. If using an iron, always iron very lightly on the wrong side using a silk setting.

Apply resist, as described on page 40, making sure that you link the paper to the puffed areas. Otherwise they just wash away. It shouldn't be necessary to apply resist to the Puff Paint – just at the edges where it joins the paper. Dissolve with water, as before. It will take a long time to dry, so be patient. Paint, using the paints of your choice, and wax, as before. If using embossing powders, be aware that heating the embossing powder may make the paint puff more. This may enhance it but could equally well spoil it. So always try a sample before using it for a great work!

A good way to design for the water-soluble technique is to use a design program on the computer. One of the plastic or enamel special effects gives a very good simulation of the way the finished paper looks, especially if metallic paints are used.

Ultra-thick embossing enamel

There have been some exciting developments in the field of rubber stamping in the past few years. The stamps themselves are of a much better design (those designed by author Sherrill Kahn are especially good) and the inks are also much improved. Embossing powders have a lot of potential for stitchers, especially the Ultra Thick powders, although these can be tricky to use on fabric. Try the following method:

Paint an area of some heavy craft Vilene (Pellon), using the smooth side of the fabric, in a suitable colour, slightly darker than the colour of the embossing powder. Use any paint or pigment ink that can be safely heated. If you find that the fabric absorbs the paint too much, try the Pebeo gel instead. While damp, sprinkle with embossing powder and heat with a heat gun to melt the

powder. Do not hold it too close or it will make holes in the fabric. Before it cools, sprinkle again with the powder and heat as before. Once more, sprinkle over the powder while still hot. Before heating again, ink a stamp (I find pigment ink is best for this) or a wooden block and have it ready to use. Heat for the third time and press the block into the hot surface when it has melted. Leave it to cool before removing the stamp. I have never found that this process damages the stamp in any way.

You should have an exciting piece that can be further enhanced by bending the Vilene (Pellon) until the surface crackles. It could also be enhanced with a very light rubbing of metallic wax and a dusting of Pearl-Ex powder.

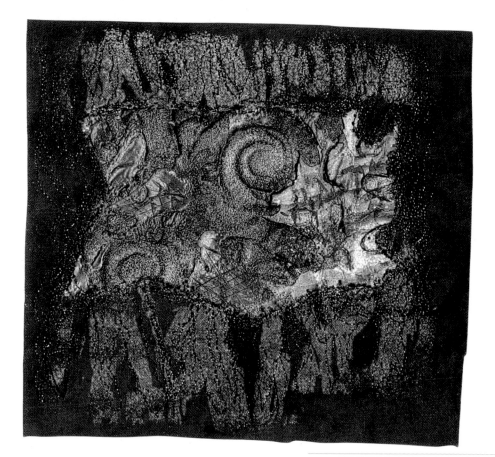

The Vilene (Pellon) surrounding the embossing powder can be stitched, as can the unembossed areas where the stamp was used. It is possible to use a form of reverse appliqué to integrate the embossing into a larger area of stitching, as follows:

1   Work on a larger piece of Vilene (Pellon). Make the embossing in the centre, or where your design dictates. You could use a temporary adhesive spray, such as 505 Spray, to hold the fabric steady while you stitch.

2   Now take the fabric to be applied – a larger piece – and cut a hole in it where the embossing is to go. Make the edges ragged, not just a precisely cut hole. Place it over the embossed area and integrate the edges of the piece with free running stitch, taking the stitching over into the painted area surrounding the embossing.

Further stitching can then be worked on the applied fabric to fully integrate the embossed area into the applied background.

Above: Embossing powder used on indigo-dyed fabric. A spiral block was impressed into the embossing powder while it was hot. Stitching was used at the edges of the piece to integrate it.
Below: Small areas of embossing can be combined. It is as well to work out a design first so you know where they are to be placed. This could be a design for a bag front.

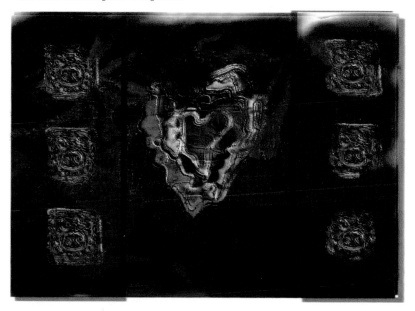

It is possible to work larger pieces by planning where on the background fabric the embossed pieces should be placed and making them all first before cutting the holes and applying the top fabric. To do this, work as follows:

1   Measure and mark out where the embossed areas will be.

2   Make these, as before, by painting the Vilene (Pellon) and then adding layers of embossing powder and heating, finishing off with the stamp. Cover the completed areas with parchment paper and a weight to prevent them from re-heating as you work. When all are complete, paint around the edges of the stamped areas with silk or fabric paints.

3   Cut fabric to cover the Vilene (Pellon). Allow an additional 1.25 cm (1/2 in) to form a seam allowance around the outer edges. Pin to the top of the Vilene (Pellon). On the reverse side, locate the stamp and push a pin through to the front. Mark with a pin on the right side just above the stamp. Do this for all the stamps. Now snip just below the pin so that you can see the stamp. Cut out just inside the edges.

4   Complete by free-machining into the stamp, as before. Add any further stitching before making into a bag, cushion, or panel.

This would also be a great technique for making brooches or bracelets where the Vilene (Pellon) could be backed with felt where it makes contact with the skin. Small geometric shapes could be linked with wire or jump rings to form the jewellery.

Opposite page: A design board showing some ideas for using embossing powders. You can see that it is possible to use reverse appliqué methods to set the stamped areas into the velvet base fabric.
Above: An embossed design formed the front of this bag, using the reverse appliqué method.
Left: Design for a bracelet.

Chapter 3
Raising the Surface a Lot

In this chapter we look at ways of adding even more texture, using beads, straws, Puff Paints, heat-reactive threads, and modelling agents. These can be combined with some of the techniques used in the last chapter, so don't be afraid to 'mix and match' when putting together a piece of work.

Materials

Artstraws are easily obtainable at art suppliers or hobby shops. They can often be found in toy shops, too. The box usually contains a mix of thin and fat straws, which is useful as the thin ones can be used to stuff the fat ones. They can be painted and textured and, as you will see, have a variety of uses.

Another range of materials that will be used in this chapter is the texture media that can be bought in art shops. A variety of these are available and they can all be used very successfully on fabric, while the addition of stitch, by hand or machine, will blend and enhance the effect.

Many of the techniques in this chapter require a heat tool – a very useful device. The heavyweight black ones are better for fabric 'zapping' than the smaller white ones.

Texture media

Look in your local art shop or hobby store to see what they have in the way of texture or gel media. The range is huge and there are exciting-sounding products such as blended fibres, rough pumice, glass beads, and moulding pastes. Gesso is often used to prepare surfaces for paint but it also works well as a texturing agent and is easily available. You can see some of the results on the luggage tags in the photograph opposite.

Materials.

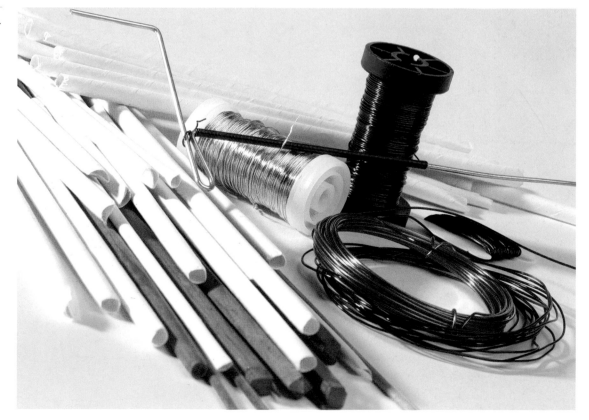

Although these substances are primarily intended for use with paints, they all work well on fabric if a firm cotton or heavy Vilene (Pellon) is used as a base. Always make a sample to test before doing a lot of stitching. The medium can be applied just as it is and painted later, or it can be mixed with paint. I prefer to paint afterwards in order to mix the colours over the entire piece.

Method

Choose one or two products (more will be confusing) and use a stout unpainted background fabric. Apply the medium using a brush or palette knife and then draw into the gel with a fork, a strip of card sideways on, a palette knife, or any interesting implement that can be used to make marks. Raid the kitchen for redundant implements (don't re-use them afterwards). The object is to make marks in the gel. Try to follow a planned design rather than just using random marks. Ensure that you have made lines for stitch in the medium as the gelled areas will be too thick to stitch through. If you use gesso, consider sprinkling it with salt while it is wet. This will dissolve later, with interesting results when paint is applied.

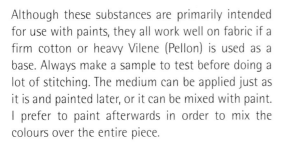

Allow to dry and add a further layer of gel if you are building a really chunky texture. When completely dry, paint with silk, watercolour or acrylic paint. Each gives different results. Allow the colours to merge as you paint but be careful not to overdo the merging or it may become muddy. Metallic wax can be used when the paint is dry to add glimmering highlights.

When all is dry, add stitching. I prefer hand stitching with a simple stitch like running stitch. Free-machine techniques can be used but take care not to stitch into the gel or you may break a needle. Use a fairly heavy yarn to make an impression – fine threads will disappear against the textured background. Run the stitches along the gaps in the gel, making sure that they enhance the design and blend in well.

Above: Embroidery based on rocks and strata using heavy gel medium. This was spread over the base fabric with the edge of a piece of card. After painting, running stitches were worked to integrate the areas. (MG)

Below: A variety of texture mediums used on fabric. They have been made into luggage tags for easy reference with the details written on the reverse of each tag.

Cut-out strips

I have always been interested in the possible uses of strips of stitching cut from felt and applied to a background. Previous books have explored this using the automatic patterns that are built into the machine. An alternative, if you don't have many patterns, is to stitch using your widest zigzag, very close together (as in satin stitch) and to pull the fabric gently from side to side as you stitch. Reduce the weight on the pressure foot if your machine lets you do this, and leave the feed-dogs up. Get into a rhythm with the stitching and make curves or points. It is possible to get good results from this method. The strips can be cut out close to the stitching and applied to a background. They could

then be outlined with machine embroidery, which raises the shape above the surface. Whip stitch (loose bobbin tension, tight top tension) could be worked around the edges in further lines of stitch.

Further experiments using wider stitched strips have been successful. Cut-out shapes give a raised effect when applied. Plan the shapes before you start. The photograph below shows a series of rectangles formed into a strip (using a satin stitch outline and free running filling). Two or more strips can be stitched and then wrapped or plaited together with beads and wrapped rings, or Flower Stitched circles could be applied. These would look great over the free-machined crochet cords described in Chapter 2.

Free-machined rectangles, stitched on felt and cut out. The strip at the bottom was made from two such strips joined together, with wrapped rings passed through one of the strips.

Close zigzag (satin) stitches are pulled
very gently to and fro (sideways) as they
are stitched. This enables an ordinary
machine with no fancy stitches to make
wider patterns. When stitched on felt,
cut out and applied with free-machining, they can be most effective. Here
they are used with hand
stitching and beads. (MG)

Making textures with layered beads

Rolled beads are often used to make jewellery but they can also be couched down on fabric to form a delightful texture. Beads can get really interesting when you start layering the materials and use a heat gun to reveal the colours below. There are many ways of making beads – here are some ideas to get you started.

Paper beads

Paper strips can be cut or torn and rolled around a knitting needle. The paper can be painted – it could be brown paper, tissue paper or drawing paper, or computer prints. There are lots of exciting papers available for computer printers, so try a variety of alternatives.

Above: Shape for bead.

Strips of fine fabric can also be treated like this. Cut long triangle shapes, wind them around a needle, starting at the wide end, and secure with a stitch or a blob of glue. Then varnish them or use a substance called Mod Podge, which gives a porcelain-like finish. Deco-Form is another such hardening product. Add some of the very tiny accent beads or glitter when the Deco-Form is wet. If white paper shows at the edge, use a fine brush to paint it.

The basic method for beads can be extended in the following ways:

- A strip of Tyvek paper (an archival paper often used for envelopes) could be painted on both sides and then wrapped around the needle on top of the paper bead. Pin in place and then zap lightly with a heat gun to reveal the coloured paper underneath. Add a little wax or gold paint to the Tyvek.

- Embossing powders could be used over an inked stamp before winding the bead.

- The long edges of the bead could be wiped along a stamp pad and embossing powder used. When the bead is wound, this gives an interesting edge.

These beads work well when they are couched to a surface, but here are three further methods for beads or tubes that can give even more exciting results.

Paper beads made from rolled, coloured paper, stiffened with Deco-Form. Small beads and glitter were added when the Deco-Form was wet. Others had stitched felt wrapped around them before zapping with a heat tool. (MG)

Zapped felt beads

To make these you will need an outer and an inner fabric. The inner fabric should be brightly coloured and fairly heat-resistant – the sort that can take quite a high iron temperature, like cotton, polycotton or, perhaps surprisingly, silk. Wrapped around this will be a strip of felt, the kind that produces a wonderful texture when zapped with a heat tool (see page 33).

Zapped felt beads, some with metallic paint.

1   Stitch a pattern on the felt using automatic patterns or hand stitching, preferably with a metallic thread. Cut into strips, perhaps 1.25 cm (¹/₂ in) wide by 2.5 cm (1 in) long.

2   Fold a twist of the brightly coloured fabric around a knitting needle and hold in place while you wrap around the strip of stitched felt fabric. Pin to hold together. Now use the heat gun (remember the mask or respirator) to zap the felt so that it clings to itself and forms a tight band around the fabric. The stitch should stand proud with some lovely texture around it, and the underneath fabric will be revealed. The beads can then be painted with gold paint or lightly coated with a metallic wax.

Beads made from light-coloured felt can resemble ivory or bone. Consider other things that could be placed in the centre – perhaps shiny beads or found objects such as shells. Painted pieces of Tyvek paper are very interesting as a bottom layer as they melt down. Remember to paint both sides. Try making very long beads that can be used to frame a central motif or form an edging. The central silk fabric could be held down by winding wire around it before wrapping with the felt. A very long bead could be used as a spacing element in a small embroidery. Try making the beads on painted kebab sticks and couching them to a background.

These beads were made from light coloured Kunin felt. They look very much like ivory. The pale colour contrasts with the richer colours below, which were revealed when the felt was heated.

Soluble paper beads

For this next method of bead making, tear rough strips of water-soluble paper, stitch them with pattern and wrap them tightly around the knitting needle. Seal with a spot of glue. Now spread some Puff Paint onto a piece of plastic (as if you were going to do a monoprint) and tap a rubber stamp into it. The flexible stamps like the Impress Me range are best for this.

Stamp onto the paper, rolling the bead over the stamp, and then use a heat tool to puff up the paint. Embossing powder could be used before heating. Sprinkle some onto the Puff Paint and heat. Don't use a resist – just splash a little water onto the paper to dissolve it and mould it into shape with another knitting needle or the end of a satay stick.

It will take some time to dry, so leave it in a warm place such as an airing cupboard or drying cabinet. When completely dry, the bead can be painted with acrylic paint, and metallic wax added when this is dry. These beads are very effective when made *in situ*, for example when forming finials on the end of painted satay sticks for book dividers or hanging mechanisms. In this case, form the bead on the end of the stick and wrap with wire to help it stick. These beads can also be formed on braids or plaits and here too they can be wrapped with wire. Make the braid first and then form the beads, one at a time. Take care when painting them so as not to get too much paint on the braid.

A concertina book with water-soluble paper beads forming the finials at the end of the wooden sticks that act as supports. Great for displaying samples, I make them when I go on workshops to remind me of the techniques used.

Nappy liner beads

Nappy (diaper) liners can make good beads when zapped with a heat gun. Not all the liners do this, so check the Resources section on pages 126–127 to see where to get them.

Paint the liners first with silk paints and then wrap them around the knitting needle. Wrap quite thickly and use a pin to hold the end in place. Now use the heat gun to distress the bead. Add wax if required, when the beads are cold. Try wrapping with fancy yarn partway through the bead, or at the end to hold it. Or wrap and pin and then wrap with a few tiny beads, threaded as a string, before continuing with more painted liner. Wire is good with these beads too as it concentrates the heat – with interesting results.

Another effect can be obtained by using a Markal (Shiva) oilstick on the strip before wrapping. This can be even more interesting if some stitching is done on the liner (use it double) first. Or wrap some painted Tyvek paper around the needle and zap lightly first. Then proceed with the nappy liner, as before.

Decorating and making beads with wire

All the beads can be wrapped with wire. It is possible to buy florists' wire in different colours and this is quite inexpensive. You can also obtain enamelled wire in some wonderful shades and a variety of thicknesses but this does tend to cost more. Wrap the wire around the bead, maybe threading on some small beads at intervals. Most

Some of the coiled-wire beads made with the Gizmo device.

Using a Gizmo device that winds wire into coils. These coils can then be used for further windings. This can also be done with a knitting needle but this cheap little device makes it easier.

wire can be wound with the fingers but the stiffer varieties may need pliers.

Wire can also be made into beads using a device called a Gizmo. This forms a tightly wound coil, which can be further adapted by making two different-sized coils and manipulating one through the other.

Consider making a long Gizmo bead with further zapped felt beads along its length. Also try dabbing the Gizmo bead with embossing ink and dipping in embossing powder. Heat as before and then thread

two pipe-cleaners through the coiled bead. Round beads can then be threaded at each end of the coil. The remaining pipe-cleaner can be wrapped with yarn and coiled into shapes or decorated with smaller beads. The book cover shown overleaf uses rows of these beads, stitched to a layered base.

Have fun making the beads. They are quite quick to make. Try making several on a painted satay stick and couching them to a background. Or make really long ones to incorporate with other elements into an embroidery.

60 Raising the Surface a Lot

The background of this book cover was made from velvet with applied crochet cords and Flower Stitch circles. Gizmo beads have been threaded with beaded and wrapped pipe-cleaners, which have been coiled into shapes and then couched onto the background.

Straws and sticks

Drinking straws can be used in conjunction with stitching for relief embroidery. Some of those offered in restaurants are often in sophisticated colours – the black ones are very sexy! However, they can be rather thick and shiny and, while they can be waxed most effectively, they tend not to take paint well. Paper straws can be bought from supermarkets but the best are those sold in art and craft shops as 'Artstraws'. It is advisable to stuff these to make them firmer – I am indebted to Siân Martin for introducing me to 'straw-stuffing'.

You will find that the Artstraws boxes contain two sizes of straws.

1   Take one of the fatter ones and cut it in half (to halve its length).

2   Take two narrow straws, cut in half as before, flatten them and fold both in half along their length.

3   Do the same with two further narrow straws and then place all four together, slotted into each other.

Straw stuffing.

4   Push the four straws down into the big one.

This should be firm enough for most purposes. If you need an even firmer straw, add more 'stuffing' straws in the same way.

When the straws are good and firm they can be painted in a suitable colour using acrylics or other such paints. If you have any texturing mediums (available from art shops), they give a good effect but should be applied before painting. Dip the ends of the straws in ink if they are hard to colour. Think about spraying or painting them gold.

Now you can consider ways of using them over a background. Here are some ideas:

● Couch them to the background. Stitch some suitably shaped strips of pattern or free-machining and apply them over the top, as in the photograph, right.

● Use a space-dyed thread and try a variety of couching stitches to secure the straw to the background. Add beads as you go.

● Stitch some interesting satin stitch patterns onto felt and cut them out. Twirl them around the straw. Use free-machine techniques if you don't have suitable patterns. Try doing this on Kunin felt and zapping it before twirling.

● Wind strips of fabric around the straw before couching.

● Place the straws vertically on the background and couch down. Now use pieces of embroidery – perhaps some that has been done on water-soluble fabric – and stitch them over and under the straws.

● Use the straws to raise motifs above a busy background and make them into a focal point.

● Wrap the straw with wire and add beads as you go along, either in a regular pattern of colour or as bursts of random beads.

● Take a chiffon sandwich and a piece of backing fabric. Stitch lines slightly wider than the straws and put a straw in each pocket. This could then be zapped to reveal the straw, parts of which could be wired and beaded.

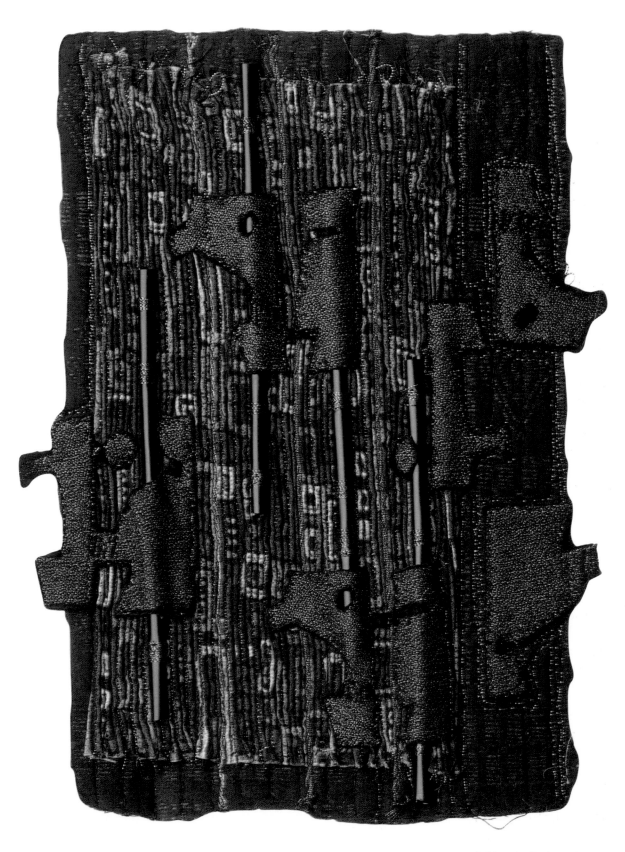

This piece by Valerie
Campbell-Harding
(16 x 26 cm/6^1/$_4$ x 10^1/$_4$ in)
used a background of a
commercial African-print
fabric that had been
pin-tucked. Black drinking
straws were couched
down, with heavily
machine-embroidered
patches applied over
the top.

Right: Straws have been painted and applied to a toning background. A large machine pattern was stitched onto Vilene (Pellon) and painted after stitching. The stitched strips were then cut out and wound around and over the straws.

Opposite page: Small pieces of fabric, heavily machine embroidered to form tiles, are stitched over painted straws. (MG)

Satay sticks and chopsticks

If something firmer than a straw is required, try using satay sticks or chopsticks. Chopsticks are often thrown in with Chinese take-away meals and are sometimes joined together at one end, which makes an interesting shape. Both the satay sticks and the chopsticks take paint well and look good when wrapped with wire and beads. They can be used to give rigidity to bags, either as part of the opening mechanism or along the sides to add shape and strength.

Making a basketweave pattern

1   Stitch the sticks horizontally to the background fabric.

2   Stitch down the wrapped cord at the top, above the top stick, and bring it down over the top two sticks.

3   Stitch down between the second and third sticks.

4   Continue in this way, taking the cord over two sticks each time, until you run out of sticks (leave the end hanging).

Top right: The background here is a commercially printed fabric with a chiffon sandwich 'zapped' over the top. Cinnamon sticks were stitched to it, then wrapped cords, made by machining over yarns, were couched down over the top, with large beads and knots forming focal points.
Right: Basketweave techniques.

5   Start a new cord and fasten it above the top stick as before. Then fasten this cord below the first stick.

6   Now take the cord over two sticks at a time, stitching down as before, to the end.

7   Continue this sequence until the sticks are covered. Varying the spacing of the cords gives different effects.

Look back at the technique described on page 55 and make some Kunin felt beads on a painted

kebab stick. Vary the inner fabric while keeping to a colour scheme. Stitch the beaded sticks to a suitable background. Intersperse with some plain sticks that have been wrapped with toning threads. Finish by weaving a cord or braid between the lines.

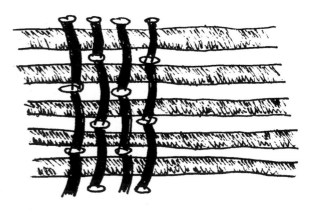

A bag with a transfer print of an icon. The sketchbook design was photocopied onto Lazertran film and then ironed onto fabric. Water-soluble fabric was stitched with metallic thread in a grid to represent the frayed patterns seen in icon paintings. The bag was constructed using two pairs of chopsticks from the take-away shop, which were beaded and wrapped with wire.

Go with the Flow (25 x 15 cm/10 x 6 in). Puff Paint was used with an adhesive spreader and 'blotted' by the fabric. After heating, it was painted with silk paints and applied to a painted background with free-machine embroidery. The stitching was heavy at the edges to merge the two together.

Fabric manipulation

Puff Paint

Very lightweight fabric can be manipulated using Puff Paint. Try the following method.

1   Roll out some Puff Paint on a glass or plastic surface. Put plenty on to make it a little thicker than usual.

2   Now use a serrated spreader, the kind sold in DIY shops for spreading tile adhesive. You can make your own from cardboard with 'teeth' cut into it, as shown in the diagram.

3   Draw the spreader through the Puff Paint, making wavy lines, and then lay a piece of sheer fabric (chiffon, georgette, or similar) on top and carefully blot to take up the Paint.

4   Allow to dry and then lay on a towel and press gently with an iron, without squashing, using a suitable temperature for the fabric. As it heats and puffs, the fabric will be drawn into an 'organic' shape.

5   Now paint the piece using silk or slightly diluted acrylic paints. The Puff Paint will probably be slightly lighter than the fabric.

6   When you are happy with the painting, prepare a suitable background – perhaps one from Chapter 1 – and pin it on, adjusting the shape and folds until you get a pleasing shape. Now use free running stitch to apply it to the background, stitching through the channels but not flattening them too much. Carry the stitch well over into the background areas at the edges to blend in the puffed piece. Finally, add some beads in the channels and dips. Another method of attaching it could be by hand stitching with running stitch in the channels.

Spreader with teeth.

Fibretex and fabric

Further fabric manipulation can be achieved using a material that shrinks, like Fibretex (a fabric-like Tyvek derivative), with one that doesn't, such as fine habotai silk.

1 Take a rectangle of Fibretex and stitch it to a piece of fine silk, leaving a narrow border of silk around the edges. Stitch in a grid, leaving quite wide areas unstitched. You shouldn't need a stabilizer because the Fibretex will support the silk, but don't worry if it pulls a little as you stitch.

2 Cut away some areas, about 1.25 cm (¹/₂ in) wide, from the Fibretex only. You are effectively taking strips out of it.

3 Snip the edges of the cut areas to encourage an interesting shape.

4 Burn the edges of the silk with a candle, working in a well-ventilated room next to a sink. Take great care.

5 Now use a heat tool to apply heat to the Fibretex. This will shrink, pulling up the silk in a ruching effect. Paint the silk with silk paints after heating. If you do it earlier, it may smoke when the heat tool is used.

6 Try other ways of stitching – grids or wavy lines – and see the effect.

Right: Fibretex, a soft form of Tyvek, is stitched to silk, using a wide grid. Areas are then cut from this before the Fibretex is treated with a heat tool.
Opposite: You can see the result of this treatment. The 'zapped' piece has been applied to a net and Angelina background.

Grilon thread

Below: Grilon samples.
Opposite top: Snippet sandwich.
Opposite right: *Paisley* (detail; 50 x 17 cm/19³/₄ x 6³/₄ in). The heat-reactive thread was used here with areas of Model Magic to create a wall hanging. An old Indian block gave texture to the Model Magic and added rectangular shapes. The pieces of manipulated fabric were used to join the blocks.

Grilon is the trade name of a heat-reactive thread. When gently heated it shrinks, and this shrinkage can be used to manipulate fabric. It can be tricky to stitch, so wind it onto the bobbin and use rayon thread in the needle. The thread can be heated with an iron to shrink it, but I am indebted to June Carroll who evolved this more-reliable method.

1   You will need a flat metal frame. These are available to purchase or can be made by bending a wire coat-hanger into a square with an overlapping fourth side. Bind the fourth side with yarn or sticky tape.

2   Wrap the Grilon thread around the frame in both directions, making sure it goes on quite densely. (If you really can't find a suitable frame, you could stitch a grid on water-soluble fabric, covering well with lots of stitching. Use Grilon on the bobbin. Frame it up, ready for free-machining.)

3   Now take your frame or wrapped square and place a variety of fabric scraps, silk tops, Angelina fibres, braids, threads, snippets, little pieces of lace etc. on top (see above).

4   Top with water-soluble fabric and then stitch with free-machine embroidery to integrate it all, still with Grilon on the bobbin. Linear stitching works well, as does a series of circles. Make sure that there is enough stitching to hold down all the loose bits but don't cover them too heavily.

5   When complete, plunge into a bowl of fairly hot water. The temperature should be slightly hotter than you can comfortably bear without gloves. If it is too hot it will destroy the Grilon. It should shrink immediately, pulling up all the stitching.

If you cannot get hold of Grilon, there is a YLI heat-reactive thread, called Fusible, which is nearly as good and which can be used in the same way.

There are lots of variations on the basic method. For example:

●   Use glitzy metallic fabric snippets mixed with dark threads for an 'old jewellery' look.

●   Stitch lightly on water-soluble fabric. Dissolve and use the light lacy pieces, with threads, on the Grilon.

●   Lay a lightweight fabric over the Grilon mesh and add threads on top.

The frame method means that quite small pieces are produced. Join them to create larger pieces of work. Combine this technique with some of the others in this book for interesting results.

June Carroll's *Beach and Two Trees* (23 x 13 cm/ 9 x 5 in) uses Grilon heat-reactive thread on water-soluble fabric. Further laid fabrics and machine embroidery add to the tex-tured effect. Small beads and hand stitching provide detail.

Carved Vilene (Pellon)

It is possible to build up texture on a firm surface, such as craft Vilene (Pellon), using crumpled tissue paper, and then to carve a surface into it with a soldering iron. This is particularly effective when placed over a painted or decorated stitched surface. Iron Bondaweb (fusible webbing) onto the Vilene (Pellon) and peel off the backing paper. While it is still hot, press the tissue into it, crumpling it as you do so, to raise the surface texture. Draw shapes onto the surface with a pencil, taking care to consider the negative, or in-between, shapes. Place the pieces on a metal tray. Burn slashes and holes in each piece with a soldering iron, taking great care not to burn your fingers. Cut into shapes, following your drawn line, and then burn the edges of the piece with a candle to give a crisp look. Burn out some extra small shapes to place on top. Now paint all these with silk or acrylic paints. Apply the shapes to the background using free-machine stitching around the edge of the shapes, then placing the smaller shapes on top and machining them in the same way. When all this is done, dab on some embossing ink and sprinkle with embossing powder. Tap off the excess and heat with a heat gun until the powder bubbles. Finish with a little metallic wax to emphasize the crinkles and folds in the paper.

A transfer-printed fabric was stitched with heavy machine embroidery using a metallic thread. On top of this is Craft Vilene, with tissue paper bonded to it, was painted before being burned with a soldering iron using an irregular pattern.

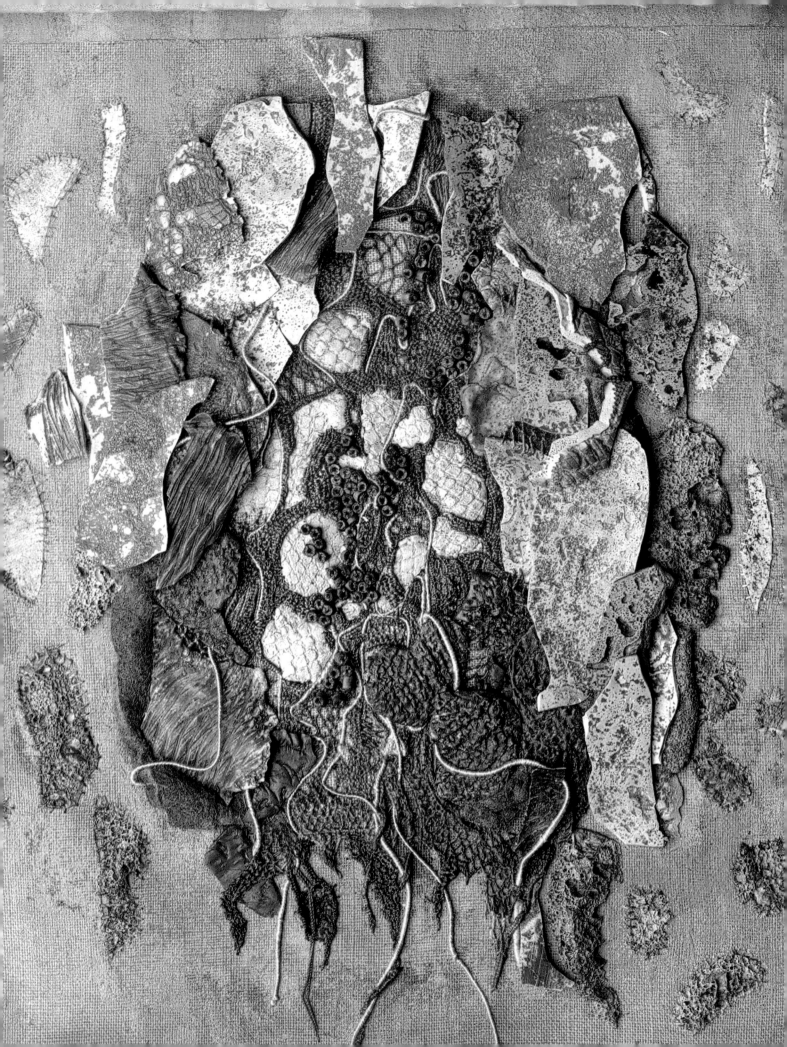

Chapter 4

Using Applied Motifs for High Relief

Some wonderful products are used to make motifs for backgrounds, ranging from the well-explored polymer clay to the newer soft modelling paste, which dries to a paper-like finish, and new uses for the glue gun. Heat-moulding foam is great for shaping, and Wireform gives tantalizing movement and lifts a flat piece of stitching. All of these give a high-relief finish to a piece of work.

Materials

Model Magic has been a favourite of mine for a very long time. It is a soft, marshmallow-like substance that can be pushed into a block or, indeed, anything with a surface texture. It will retain the texture and can then be air-dried, painted, waxed, and stitched to a backing fabric ready for further stitching.

The humble hot-glue gun can be a formidable ally in embroidery. Used with rubber stamps or just to draw freehand shapes, it can produce delightful translucent effects. These can be painted or waxed, used directly on fabric or applied afterwards.

For many three-dimensional effects, I find that a heat-moulding foam is very effective. This is sometimes called Softsculpt or Formafoam. It is easy to cut with scissors and can be gently heated before being pressed into a shape. Impressions can be made into the foam to add to the decorative effect. The thicker version of this foam works best for these effects.

Polymer clay in the form of Fimo or Sculpey can really add high-relief effects to embroidery. Inexpensive and easily obtainable, it can be layered, moulded, and crackled to produce effects that range from ancient metal to crumbly stone. The trick here is to find the best way to attach it to the fabric and combine it with stitch. Several of these avenues are explored here.

Wireform, a wire mesh, can safely be stitched with a sewing machine. It comes in a range of weights, which makes it suitable for many purposes. Sandwiched between two layers of fabric, it is the ideal material to make a background for applied motifs. It can also be used for cuffs and masks, and makes good vessels. Being lightweight, it adds no bulk to an item.

Previous page: *Earth Jewels* by Margaret Gamble (33 x 33 cm/13 x 13 in). Polymer clay pieces were trapped by embroidery and wrapped wires in this elegant composition. Some of the clay shapes have been joined using faggoting stitches. **Right**: Wireform, Model Magic and paints.

Detail of *Fossil Layers* (page 7). Model Magic was used with a fossil to produce a high-relief piece of embroidery.

Model Magic

Model Magic is a very versatile modelling material that is easily moulded in its soft, natural state. It is then allowed to air-dry and can be painted, stitched and incorporated into embroideries. Lots of things can be used as a moulding surface for the material. I had great success with a fossil that had both a positive and negative image on which to press the material. Using the material in workshops has seen the entire class communing with trees as they pressed the Model Magic into the bark. The fact that some of the bark remained attached just added to the texture. So be adventurous when looking for surfaces. Any sensitive surface can be covered with Clingfilm (plastic wrap) to protect it.

To use Model Magic, break off a small piece, work it in your hand for a short while and then press it into a suitable mould (the mould can be lined with Clingfilm [plastic wrap] first). This could be a fossil, a printing block, carved wood, or anything else with sufficient depth to make an impression. Very carefully, peel away from the mould, lay on a flat surface, and allow to dry for 24 hours. Make sure that the remainder of the modelling material is wrapped in Clingfilm (plastic wrap) and sealed in airtight containers. When the shaped piece is dry, it can be painted. It accepts most paints quite happily: acrylics, fabric paints, even inks and watercolours. Allow it to dry and then varnish with matt varnish or use clear embossing ink and embossing powders around the base of the shape. This strengthens it ready for stitching. Waxes and/or Pearl-Ex powders can be used too.

Now for the stitching. It is essential that these three-dimensional elements are bedded into the work. Proper integration is a must or they will just look 'plonked down'. Prepare a background using any of the methods described in Chapter 1.

Hand stitch the motifs in place using strong thread and, just attaching around the edge, bring the thread up outside the motif and take it down through it. Do not pull the thread too tightly when stitching into Model Magic or it will pull right through the paper-like material (this is where the embossing powder is helpful). When the piece is attached, it is time to consider further stitching tactics, which could be hand or machine or a mixture of both. Here are just a few ideas:

The fossils here have been used to impress a design into the Model Magic.

- Use silk paper in folds to form waves around the forms.

- Use hand and machine stitching, taking the machining up to, but not into, the motif. The photograph, right, shows hand stitching, which has had free-machining worked on top of it right up to the applied pieces. The machine stitching over hand stitching gives good cover.

- When making the motif, run little 'spurs' or strips of Model Magic out from it and stitch by hand around them. Heavy couched threads could be used to cover the spurs, and further stitching into these will help to bed-in the piece.

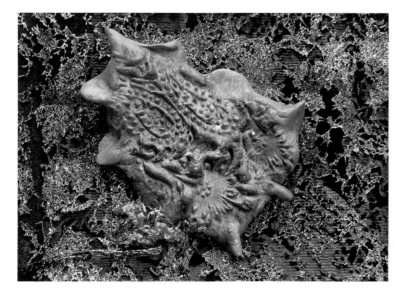

Above: The impressed Model Magic was painted and gilded with metallic wax. It was then set into a piece of commercial silk paper and hand stitched. Care was needed to bring the fabric over the top of the impressed design to cover the edges.
Left: Model Magic, which has been pressed into a fossil and painted, is placed on a chiffon sandwich background. The little spurs on the edges of the motif are covered with thick yarn and then stitches are taken up from the background to attach it. Lots of stitching is needed to integrate the fossil piece. (MG)

Glue gun

Use an ordinary hot-glue gun on non-stick parchment paper to make delicious flowing motifs to apply. **Be aware that the glue is very, very hot. Do not touch it until it cools.** You could draw a freehand shape on the non-stick paper or stamp an impression on it with a wooden block or rubber stamp and an ink pad. It's a little tricky following the lines of the stamp with the gun but a wobble or two adds character and frees up the shape. It's also possible just to draw with the glue gun, without a guide. Raise the gun and stretch the strands of glue very thinly to make wispy lines. It's a bit like icing a cake or using spun sugar – great fun.

This fluid shape has been made with a glue gun and waxed to give a metallic effect. Couching techniques were used to attach it to a painted ground fabric. The whole is framed with painted straws decorated with a smaller glue motif. (MG)

Think about adding beads to the hot clay by dropping them on while it is hot. **Do not touch it at this stage or you will burn your fingers.** Squirting glue into a bowl of cold water will produce a very exciting lace-like motif.

Glue can be added to a motif made from embossing powders (page 44) where it will add height. It is especially good for redeeming disasters. You could also prepare a base by building up a thick layer of ultra-thick embossing powder, sprinkling it with a coloured embossing powder and melting it to get a marbled effect. Allow to cool and then use the glue gun over the top. See the suggestions overleaf for colouring.

Stamping

You can use a glue gun directly with a rubber stamp. It does sometimes stick, so don't use your best stamps. The stamp needs to be placed in the glue when it is warm rather than hot (as it is to begin with). Let the glue get really cool, then gently warm it. The following method works well.

1   Use the glue gun as before on non-stick parchment paper to make a 'glue patch'. Don't make it too thick or it will look heavy. I like a fragmented look so I leave some holes. Allow to cool.

2   Now use a heat gun for a short time, just until the glue starts to lose its shape. Have ready an inked stamp and press it into the warm glue. Allow the glue to cool completely before removing the stamp.

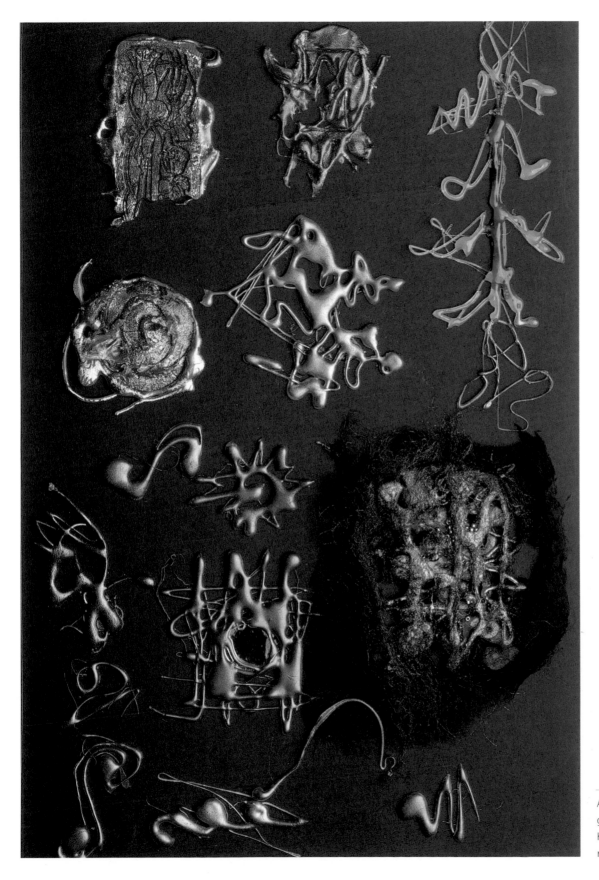

A design board showing glue gun samples that have been coloured with metallic wax.

Colouring

When the glue motifs have been made (by either method) and cooled, they can be painted with acrylic paints. However, my preferred method is to use a metallic wax. Use your finger to rub the wax over the surface, as you can reach all the nooks and crannies this way. Some waxes are almost translucent and give a very light, transparent effect. You can make your own wax by mixing two parts of hard silicone furniture polish with one part bronze powder. **Always wear a mask when using bronze powders.** This wax will keep for a week or two if it is sealed, so make it in small quantities. While the wax application is fresh, use powders like Pearl-Ex to give a lovely sheen. Just dust the powder over the top with a brush.

An alternative method of gilding is to apply the glue straight onto foils. These are sheets of metallic film that can be rubbed off over special glue or even fusible webbing (as used in the chiffon sandwiches). The glue should be used on the non-shiny side of the foil. Peel away when cold and you will find that the base of the glue motif is covered with the foil, and very shiny. To knock it back, heat for a short time and then press a stamp into it. That will break it up a little but it will probably still be too shiny, so rub with a little dark wax or a dry brush of dark acrylic paint for an aged look.

Stitching

It is, of course, possible to make the motifs directly on fabric but this makes it difficult to colour them unless you paint the fabric too. This can work well and is worth a try.

One method I particularly favour is to use the glue gun on the paper parchment and then place a piece of fine chiffon over the top while it is hot. **Do not touch the hot glue while doing this.** Allow to cool, turn over and colour the glue. It is easy to

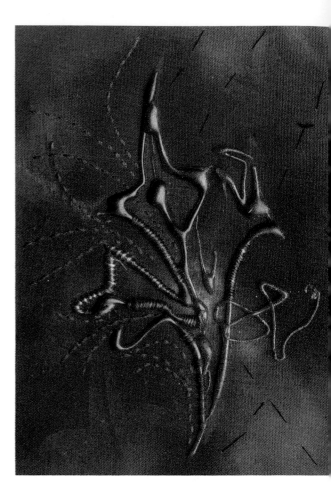

attach to a background by stitching the fabric. This can be taken further by adding more layers of glue and chiffon and sprinkling in some beads. Finish with a layer of glue. This can be lightly toasted with a heat gun to distress the chiffon but beware of melting too much of the glue.

Glue motifs can also be hand stitched by couching to the base fabric, which offers more control of the colour and placement. I normally use a toning space-dyed thread and couch down the narrower areas. I also take a few stitches through the body of the glue motif but this is not easy and can make your needle sticky. Once attached, further embroidery can be added around the motif by hand or machine.

As previously mentioned, there are some software packages suitable for textile design that have special effects. Some of these are great for generating ideas to use with glue-gun motifs. These are often called 'Melted Plastic' or 'Enamel'.

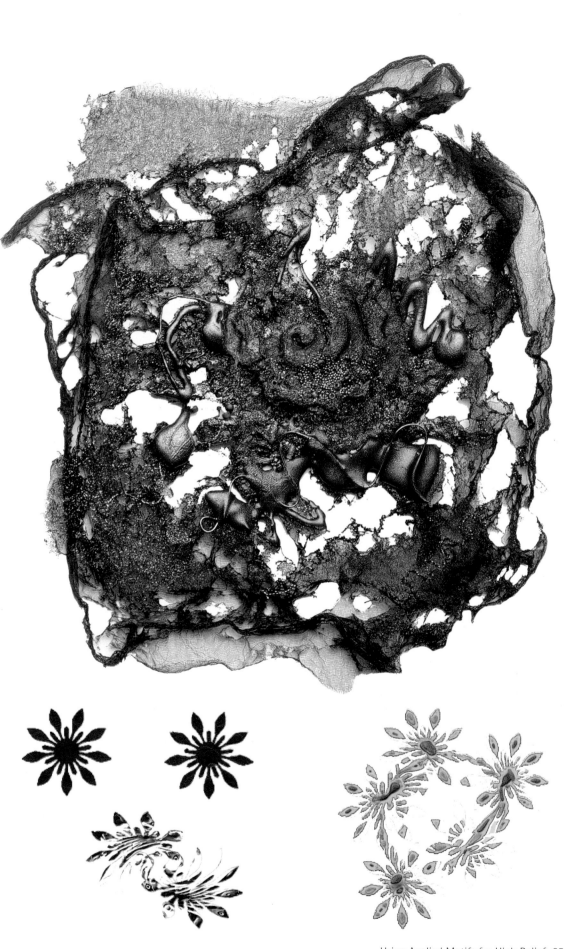

Far left: This partly stitched piece shows a background of painted fabric. A foam block was printed over this and the same block was used as a design for the glue motif. This was then waxed and couched to the background fabric with hand stitching.

Left: Glue with layers of chiffon and beads. The glue was waxed and the chiffon 'zapped' with a heat tool.

Below: The effects of computer-generated enamel filters.

Softsculpt

Softsculpt, or Formafoam, is a heat-mouldable foam that can be formed into shapes while it is hot. Follow the instructions on the pack and do not overheat the material.

It can be used to make three-dimensional additions to panels. The photograph below shows a torso shape cut from the foam and then textured.

Cut out the required shape from the foam, heat with a heat gun and mould by just pushing it with your hands to add a three-dimensional aspect.

Assemble a variety of materials onto glue to the shape. These could include short lengths of string, nails, slivers of wood, pieces of machine embroidery, or almost anything. Use a glue gun or contact adhesive to stick them to the foam.

When dry and firmly fixed, apply a coat of PVA glue all over the surface. Before it dries, press tissue paper all over it, being careful to press it into all the nooks and crannies made by the texture elements. Don't stretch the tissue too much; crinkle it slightly to make further texture. When dry, repeat the process with another layer of tissue paper. Take it round to the back of the piece, too. This is a messy stage, so keep a pack of wipes handy.

Making the textured torsos featured opposite.
Left: a glue gun was used to stick a variety of textures to thick foam. Pieces of wood, nails, and string were all used.
Right: When the glue was dry, the whole piece was coated with PVA glue and tissue paper pressed into the textured areas. This was then ready for painting

When all is completely dry, paint with acrylic paints using one or two colours. It looks most effective if a metallic wax is applied when the paint is dry, especially if a dark colour has been used for the painting. My torso pieces featured here were based on a bronze sculpture.

The piece can be applied to a stitched background, using a big needle and taking it up from the backing and down through the work. Make sure that the backing is firmly stabilized or it will buckle.

Look out at car-boot (garage) sales for suitable items to use for shaping. I had great success pressing foam over a heart-shaped candle and then applying a suitable stitched design to it. It was mounted over a background made up of straight-stitch lines and then framed using board with a heart-shaped cut-out to allow it to stand proud of the frame. (This piece can be seen on page 100.)

Before the Fall 1 and *2* (38 x 30 cm/15 x 12 in). The completed male and female torsos, which were painted with black acrylic paint and copper metallic wax, were applied to a stitched velvet background. A border of dried leaves, trapped in chiffon, was gilded with metallic waxes in rich colours.

Design ideas for using polymer clay. *Top left* Painted polymer with black acrylic under gold paint for an old metal effect. *Centre* Pieces of the clay wrapped around a kebab stick, ready to apply to fabric. *Right* Various methods for attaching to fabric. Fromtop to bottom: Clay placed on metal mesh; Clay with Lazertran image and holes for stitching; Clay on Wireform with silk paper ready to be stitched over it.

Polymer clay

Polymer clay is available in so many colours that it is difficult to decide which to choose. I like the Fimo clay that looks like stone and I find that layering it with a darker-coloured clay gives interesting results.

Work with fairly small pieces by pulling off a piece of clay and rolling it between your fingers until it is pliable, and then flatten it with a small rolling pin or just using finger pressure. Make two pieces like this from the stone colour and one from a darker plain shade.

Sandwich the plain colour between the stone ones, keeping the top layer quite thin. Press the layers together. Tear a strip from the clay, about 2 cm (3/4 in) wide and about 7 cm (2 1/2 in) long. Tearing it gives a good edge. Wrap one end around a painted kebab stick so that it overlaps a little at the back. Press the overlap so that it adheres to itself and attaches to the stick.

Now use a heat tool on the top for a short time, not allowing it to get too hot. This will form a crust on the clay which can be accented further by gently bending it to encourage cracks to form. Make more tiles like this, attaching them to the stick.

Some could be impressed by using a stamp or block while the clay is soft. It works best by only using part of a stamp (rubber ones are good for this as they bend). This looks like part of an eroded carving. When the stick has the required number of tiles, place it in an oven, at the temperature suggested on the pack and for the time stated. Do not overheat. Apply it to fabric by stitching the stick to the base fabric, either using couching stitches in contrasting colours, or blending it in by using coloured thread that disappears into the background.

An alternative for using the polymer clay could be to make tiles with holes at the corners, which are created by pushing a skewer through the clay before baking. This would make them easy to stitch onto fabric. Embossing powder, especially the stamped version described on page 44, works well on Fimo. Use it after baking the clay.

If you can lay hands on an old pasta machine, this will add to the effects that can be produced with

Polymer clay tiles were painted before being lashed to painted satay sticks. These, in turn, were stitched to a PC transfer-paper background.

clay. Keep it just for clay – don't use for food afterwards. With this machine, you can roll out really thin sheets that almost fall to bits and can be heaped up on a previously textured clay shape. Press lightly and bake.

Texture gels and paint could be used after baking. A really good effect can be obtained by using Lazertran paper to transfer a design onto the clay. Take your design to the copy shop and have them transfer it to the Lazertran paper. (Make sure they use the colour copier, even if the design is black-and-white.) Follow the pack instructions for making a permanent transfer to the clay using the

turpentine method, where the acrylic film is floated off the backing, placed on the clay, and painted with turpentine when it is dry. This could be wonderful for portraying old frescos as the transfer can be distressed by rubbing with a paintbrush at the soft and jelly-like stage.

Be inventive by considering the methods that could be used to stitch the tiles to the background. Refer to the section on 'Straws and sticks' in Chapter 3 (page 62) and see how the clay could be adapted to work with these. Some ideas are suggested in the diagrams below.

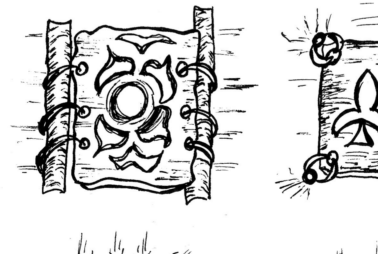

Right: Ways of attaching Fimo clay.
Opposite: Wireform purse by Margaret Beal. Wireform was sandwiched between synthetic fabrics. A fine-tipped soldering iron was used to make decorative marks on the fabrics before the sides were joined to form the purse. The Wireform gave it an interesting shape and provided the rigidity.

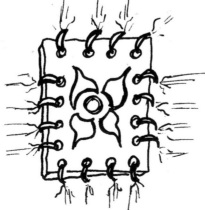

Wireform

Wireform is a sheet of fine wire that can be sandwiched between fabric and stitched using an ordinary domestic sewing machine. It can then be bent into shape and used for a variety of purposes. It adds movement to a piece and can be formed into different shapes, from a subtle ripple to a vessel or box (more on that aspect in Chapter 6). If you plan a lot of movement or are using a heavy fabric then use one of the heavier weights of Wireform. For light fabrics and a little manipulation the lighter weight will be fine. Wireform is hard on the hands and can easily scratch or cut you, so be very careful, especially when cutting it.

To add relief to a surface, it is best to use one large or several small manipulated pieces on a prepared background. Do this by sandwiching the wire between fabrics (lighter-weight fabric is best). The edges can be neatened or left frayed.

To make tidy edges, turn the edges of one piece over the Wireform to the reverse and then place the backing fabric over them, tucking the edges of this neatly to the inside all round and tacking as you go. Then stitch all over, either using random stitching or following a planned design. Manipulate into shape before stitching to the background. To get a tight curl, roll the corners around a pencil, rolling towards the middle. This works well with a

Left: Wireform motif with wrapped wire edges coiled into spirals then placed on a strippy stitched background.

square and the curls could be bridged at the centre with a Gizmo bead or some such device.

Lots of small versions of these could be made instead and fastened with beads. Use your imagination and try lots of variations – but be aware that the lighter-weight Wireform will break if it is bent and unbent too often.

Chapter 5

Frames, Masks and High-relief Embroidery

We now look at some rather different ideas for making frames for your work. Masks and techniques for incorporating a three-dimensional element into wall hangings are covered. High-relief wall panels can create interesting shapes and much can be made of the shadows they produce.

Materials

Many of the materials used in this chapter have been covered earlier in the book. Frames and masks can be made from the heat-moulding foam, Softsculpt, which gives a good base shape for a variety of techniques. Wireform can also be used for a base shape or could form part of the work itself. Friendly Plastic makes a good decorative element. Finally, the humble plastic canvas can be transformed into an exciting material for frames or high-relief constructions using a very simple technique.

Frames

In Chapter 4, many different materials, from string to old nails, were used to make texture by laminating foam with PVA glue and tissue paper. This principle can be extended to making frames with plastic canvas. Stitching can be done with string on the canvas before it is covered with tissue. Here is the basic method.

Materials: Wireform, plastic canvas, Friendly Plastic and clip-frames.

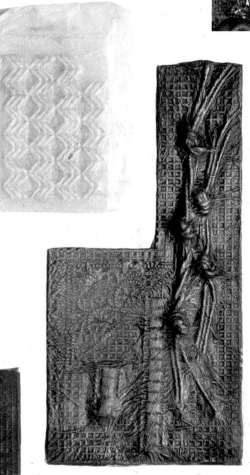

Plastic canvas frames

Cut a piece of plastic canvas to the size required for the frame. Cut the same size in mountboard to support the plastic. You will also need a backing board, which could be a piece of hardboard, cut to size, or, for a heavier effect, try a piece of MDF (medium-density fibreboard). You can sometimes find clip-frames very cheaply in surplus stores and these are great if you can get the right size. They also have glass cut to the frame size and this can be useful if a glazed piece is required.

Cut a hole towards the centre of the canvas in the exact place where the embroidery is to go. Check this by placing the embroidery on the backing board, put the canvas on top and mark where the hole goes. Place it so that there is slightly more mount at the bottom than at the top. Cut exactly the same-size hole in the mountboard.

You will need string (not yarn as it's too soft) and a needle that will take the string and not be too big to pull through the canvas. Thread up the needle and begin to stitch into the canvas. You may need to refer to a canvaswork book but some basic stitches – cross stitch for instance – are easy to work. Do not use anything too complex, or too raised a stitch. I find that cushion stitch or some of the cross stitches are ideal. Start the stitching by leaving a long end and catching it under the stitching as you go. You don't need to worry too much about this as the glue will hold it all together. Finish by taking the string under a few stitches at the back. Try to plan the stitching beforehand, if you are doing a regular pattern, so that you don't wind up at the end with an odd number of holes. Initially it may be easier to make a random pattern. The cheat's way to do it is to stitch the plastic canvas first and then cut to the approximate size after the pattern is stitched. The edges of the canvas and the central hole can be overstitched to great effect.

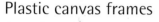

Top left: Plastic canvas stitched with string. **Top right:** Tissue applied with PVA glue. **Below left and right:** Result after painting and gilding.

Left: Plastic canvas with tied string couched to it. This was covered with two layers of tissue before finishing with paint and metallic wax. The top right of the sample shows where a figured plastic tablecloth was trapped below the tissue.

Cut two pieces of tissue paper, at least 8 cm (3 in) bigger all around than the plastic. When all the stitching is complete, place the canvas on the piece of board and then put it all on non-stick parchment paper. Spread PVA glue all over the canvas, using a large brush. Make sure that all areas are covered but do not put the glue on too thickly or allow it to pool. Then place one sheet of tissue over the top, working small areas at a time and pressing the tissue right into the string. Don't stretch the tissue over the stitching or it will tear – it needs to touch canvas or string all over the frame. This is a rather sticky process, so put on the answering machine and keep some wipes handy. Repeat this with the second piece of tissue, again pressing really well into the contours of the stitch. The second piece is not nearly so sticky. Do not cut away the excess paper around the edge. Leave it all to dry completely. Make sure that the tissued canvas is well stuck to the mountboard. Add more glue if necessary. Cover with parchment paper and leave it under a pile of books so that it is well stuck down.

The fun part can now begin – painting the canvas frame. Do this before putting it together. The paints could be acrylics in bright colours, permanent inks, or strong watercolours. Whichever paint you use, try to blend the colours to avoid jarring changes. This is easier with acrylics as they merge together nicely, so they may be a good starting point. Ink could be used, although the lack of colour-fastness may be a problem. The inks that can be discharged (usually called fountain-pen ink) give lovely effects when a little bleach is used over them. I have found that, where these do fade, it is very slight and the fading can add an attractive bronze tinge.

I like to use metallic shoe polish or wax very lightly over the top of the colour, as this brings out the texture of the stitch and helps to blend colours where more than one is used. Be very sparing with

the wax; a light touch will give better results. If the worst happens and a 'blob' occurs, just paint over it and re-wax when it is dry.

To complete the frame, cut the inner opening so that there is enough tissue to fold to the back of the mountboard. Glue down at the back, making sure that the tissue on the fold is well glued.

When this is dry, position the embroidery on the backing board. Secure with double-sided tape or fabric adhesive. The stitched piece should be larger than the frame opening, with no gaps showing. Place the canvas and board in the correct position over the frame. Paste the tissue that overlaps the edges of the frame, one layer at a time, and bring them to the back of the frame. Cover every bit with PVA glue, as it is this that makes the tissue strong. Paste the next layer and bring around over the top. Tape over the edges to neaten the back. You can glaze the work by placing glass, cut to size, directly over the stitching and using wide tape to secure it to the backing board. Then place the frame on top and continue as before.

Above: *Faded Angel* (20 x 17cm/8 x 6³/4 in). The frame is made by the plastic canvas method. Areas were cut away from the frame to allow the fabric below to show through. The central motif was made from fine metal shim with a Lazertran design applied to it.
Left: Detail of *Faded Angel*.
Far left: The central area of a frame is cut out ready for folding back and gluing at the rear of the canvas.

Left: Beaded book cover, plastic canvas with string stitching. Pearly paint was applied on the tissue, followed by counted thread stitching and beads. Button-hole stitch on the edges.
Right: *Cosmic Breath* (30 x 20 cm/12 x 8 in). Heat moulding foam was used for the frame. To enhance the Indian theme, a small carved sandalwood box was used to make impressions in the foam. The embroidery was applied on top and stitched to the foam.

That is the basic method, but there are lots of possibilities for extending this technique. For example:

- Use crumpled brown paper instead of tissue. This can have a surprising difference. The crumpling makes it soft and pliable, so work it in your hands until it is very floppy. Take care not to tear it, though. Painted Bondaweb (fusible webbing) could be ironed onto it before sticking it to the canvas, as described in Chapter 1. If you do this, do not stitch on the canvas. Keep it plain.

- Cut additional holes in the plastic canvas and prepare some small pieces of embroidery to fit into them. They should, of course, be sympathetic to the main piece of stitching.

- Lengths of string could be knotted along their length and attached to the plastic canvas by taking the odd stitch across them. These look great when the tissue is laminated over them. Take care to press the tissue well into the join of string and canvas. Try trapping pieces of lace, braid, or anything that has a texture. (A shop near me sells horrible raised-plastic tablecloths that are wonderful for trapping.)

- When everything is quite dry, more stitching could be worked over the top of the painted canvas using the visible grid as a basis for canvaswork stitches. Beads could be attached at this time, too.

- Instead of using this method to make an entire frame, use plastic canvas strips, stitched and laminated, along the sides of a piece of work, to add a finishing touch. This works particularly well with unframed pieces that are mounted on MDF or wood, as the sides are quite thick and require some sort of finish. I often use fancy-headed nails to secure the strips.

Making frames from heat-moulding foam

We have used heat-moulding foam to make pieces to apply to a background but the fact that the foam can take impressions and can be stitched makes it very suitable to be used as a frame.

Impressions can be made in it by heating an area with a warm iron for a several seconds (use non-stick parchment paper between the foam and the iron) or with a heat tool and, very quickly, pressing a hard stamping block into the foam. **Do not overheat as this can cause dangerous fumes.**

Move to a new area of the foam, using a piece of fabric or paper to mask the area you have just processed. Do not get this part hot or it will go flat. You can re-heat several times to get it right. I used the lid of a wooden Indian box to texture the foam in the photograph, right.

It was cut to shape first. After the impressions were made, metallic wax was used to give the appearance of worked metal. A strip of foam was wound around a pencil and heated before it was stitched to the base. Then a suitable piece of free-machined work (based on an Indian motif) was hand stitched to the foam frame. It was a little light, so it was glued with contact adhesive to a wooden backing, slightly smaller than the frame.

Open Hearted and Broken Hearted. Two small heart-shaped embroideries with a base of heat-moulding foam. A heart-shaped candle was used as a mould and the frames were covered with Bondaweb (fusible webbing) on brown paper.

Look out at car-boot (garage) sales for suitable items to use for shaping. In the photographs above, the foam was moulded over a heart-shaped candle and then had a suitable stitched design applied to it. It was mounted over a background made up of straight-stitch lines and then framed using board with a heart-shaped cut-out to allow it to stand proud of the frame.

Endless possibilities exist for taking this further. Small, textured pieces of foam could be stitched together, overlapping them with embroidery, either as a centre or mixed among the foam pieces. Alternatively, squares or rectangles could be joined using insertion stitches around the embroidery.

It is the fact that the foam is so easy to stitch that is exciting here. Additions can be stitched on top, and these could take the form of further textured or twisted pieces of foam, large beads, pieces of soft metal shim, or polymer clay. It is also easy to add tassels and other appendages to the frames.

Making frames from foam-board

This thick, light board can have fabric stretched over it and is useful because it is light and quite tough. It has a particular part to play where layers of board are required. In the pieces shown here, several layers were shaped, cut and stuck together before stitched fabric was stretched over the board and secured at the back. It has advantages in that it can be cut into quite intricate shapes.

In this shaped frame and clock (two pieces 23 x 18 cm/ 9 x 7 in each), Jennie Pickering used a paint program to produce pleasing spiral shapes. These were digitised using the Bernina Artista software and stitched onto hand-dyed silk organza. This was applied to silk, stitched with decorative patterns. The fabric was then mounted on foam board and edged with spiral braid and cord.

Masks

I find that the best way to produce interesting masks is to make them in two pieces – otherwise you end up with a 'Lone Ranger' effect. Cutting a pattern from a sheet of A4 paper is a good idea.

Mask layout.

Work out how the pieces are going to fit together. Ask the following questions:

- Do I need to see through the mask? (If not, don't worry about getting the eyes level.)

- Is the mask to extend above (headdress) or below eye level?

- Are fabrics or textures to be applied? (If so, keep a more simple shape.)

- Could I build up a shape using further pieces of material applied to a base? (If so, decide on the basic shape first.)

- Can I build up areas of texture using the glue-gun, string and tissue technique?

Making masks from heat-moulding foam

Forming a mask on a plastic shaper. The warm foam was quickly pressed onto the shaper. You can also see a partly painted mask that was made using the laminated tissue method.

A suitable material for masks is the heat-moulding foam that we have been using throughout the book. You will need a head or face shape to mould it over. This could be a polystyrene or plastic head, such as is used to display wigs or hats and can often be purchased from a shop-fitting company. Alternatively, you will find that many of the companies selling the heat-moulding foam will be able to supply plastic shapers such as the one shown in the photograph. Then proceed as follows.

1 Draw out the basic shape for the mask and cut out the necessary number of pieces from the heat-moulding foam.

2 Place them over the shaper to see exactly where they will need to be placed to achieve the correct shape.

3 Heat them one at a time, using an appropriate heat source. An electric oven is best for this but an iron will work too. Don't overheat. Very quickly, place the pieces in position on the shaper and press down firmly. If a bit goes wrong, just re-heat and try again – lots of second chances.

4 When they are all formed, stitch them together in the mask shape if it is sensible to do so. Some methods of decoration are better done with the mask in its separate shapes, and then joined afterwards.

Mask made using heat-moulding foam with some areas embossed by pressing a shape into the warm foam. Intricate surfaces have been formed using the laminated tissue method with black acrylic paint and metallic wax.

Frames, Maks and High-Relief Embroidery 103

A Wireform mask covered with wisps of chiffon sandwich gives a light, ethereal look. Friendly Plastic was formed and stitched to the mask for highlights. The silvery mesh of the wire shows through the chiffon.

Using Wireform for masks

It is quite possible to use Wireform for the base of the mask. Use one of the heavier weights or use two layers of the finer wire and machine the covering fabric to the wire before shaping. Follow the suggestions on the previous page for designing the shape. Press the wire onto the face mould to get the shaping right. Be aware that the edges are very sharp – you could perhaps fold them under or bind them once the basic shape is decided. Two-piece masks can be made from the wire, too. Think about the decorating ideas on the facing page, but bear in mind that the stitching should be done first. If the wire is to show through, which can be attractive, consider spraying it first with a metallic spray paint. If the mask is to be worn, it should be well lined with a thin layer of wadding between the wire and lining to protect the face.

Decorating the mask

At the most basic level, all you need to do is paint the foam mask with acrylic paint and/or metallic wax. However, one of the best things about a mask is the fact that you can go totally over the top and have the most enormous fun decorating it. Here are some suggestions:

- Apply sheer fabrics using a glitzy thread to stitch them to the foam or wire. Use beads, couched cords or ribbons over the top.

- Place a metallic net over the mask and then add beads in the centre of each grid.

- Prepare a richly embroidered fabric and stitch to the base. Add feathers.

- Make strips of heat-moulding foam and wrap them around a pencil or wooden-spoon handle. Use a heat gun on them, taking care not to overheat. Make chunky ones and very fine ones. Colour with wax and apply to the foam or wire.

- Before assembling the mask, build up areas of texture with string etc. as described on page 86. (For Wireform, cover with tissue paper first as a base.) Join the pieces together after covering with tissue and painting. Use a strong needle and thread for the joining and wear a thimble, if necessary, to push the needle through. Finish with metallic wax.

Foam mask made in two main pieces, stitched together after shaping. A chiffon sandwich was applied and couched down with straight stitches and beads. Three leaf-shaped pieces of foam were twisted and applied to the top of the mask.

Decorating with Friendly Plastic

A really exotic covering could be made with Friendly Plastic, which is sold in craft shops and is often used to make rather grim jewellery. A far better method was pioneered by Liz Welch and it can be used on its own to form masks. I use it as a decoration over the top of the foam or wire, making it on paper parchment for each section of the mask and then applying it afterwards. To do this try the following:

1   Draw the shape of the area that you are covering on the parchment paper. This will be the shape of your mask pieces. Cut narrow rectangles across the strip of plastic and place them around the area drawn. It is best to use two or three colours. Place strips close together around the edge of the shape to define it but spread them out over the inner area to keep it light and lacy.

2   Use a heat gun on a small area of plastic. Next, using an embossing tool or old knitting needle to dip into the plastic, pull over a strand to the next rectangle where it should be pressed in to make it stick. Dipping the needle into cold water or a little oil first will prevent it sticking. Work across all the plastic in this way until the area is finished. If it cools, warm it up again with the heat tool. Continue until all the mask pieces have been worked.

3   To apply to the mask, first decide if the foam, which will act as the base, needs a little metallic wax or paint. If so, do this first. Wire bases just need a layer or two of sheer fabrics stitched on them. Then turn the plastic pieces over (place them on parchment paper) and heat for a short time until they are just shiny. Lift the piece, using the parchment paper, and place it on the mask. Press the plastic so that it sticks to the base. (Place your hand behind the mask to help with the pressure but be careful that it is not too hot to touch.) Continue to apply the plastic to the mask until the decoration is complete.

Small scraps of fabric or beads can be pushed into the plastic when it is hot. Obviously this must be done before attaching to the foam.

Warning! Remember not to use a heat tool on the basic foam mask or it will lose its shape.

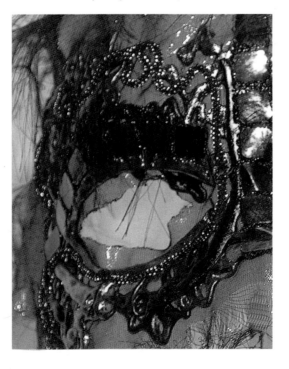

Right: Detail of Liz Welch mask. The Aztec theme is depicted in the small mosaic-like squares of Friendly Plastic.
Above right: Small pieces of Friendly Plastic are laid out on baking paper. They are then heated with a heat tool before a needle or skewer is used to manipulate the soft plastic. The result will overlay a Softsculpt mask.

The delicate *Winter Mask* by Liz Welch has a base of Friendly
Plastic applied to silver organza and net. Strings of tiny
Friendly Plastic beads and stars add an ethereal elegance.

Frames, Masks and High-Relief Embroidery 107

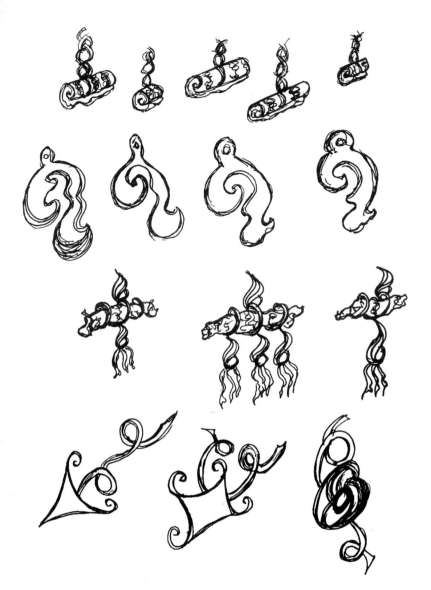

especially if the clear glossy plastic is used. Remember to make holes before heating with a hole punch, top and bottom, to allow a narrow cord to be threaded through. Lots of these could be made and threaded on cords for the mask danglies.

Strips of Wireform could have fabric stitched over them and then be rolled around a cord. The edges of the strips could be covered with narrow satin stitch. Alternatively, torn strips of fabric could be used, which would give an informal appeal. Try heat-moulding foam in strips wound around pencils and heated. Glue guns, too, can be used to form lovely shapes and they can be applied directly onto the cord. Fimo (polymer clay) could be impressed on the back and the front and could then be formed directly on the cord or have holes made before painting.

Poles for masks

Smaller masks could be attached to sticks or poles. The weight of the stick should be appropriate to the size of the mask. Although the heavier type of kebab stick is fine for narrow masks, a visit to the DIY shop may be called for if a larger mask is planned. The pole could be painted or wrapped with fabric before additional decoration is added. This could take the form of zapped strips of stitched felt, beaded yarn, and so on. Link the decoration of the stick to the decoration on the mask so that it all hangs together.

Appendages for masks

Masks can be decorated with appendages.

Lots of the techniques for beads that were covered in Chapter 3 will work well here too. Think of the paper beads, those made with nappy liner or zapped felt. Gizmo-made coils, too, could be used here. String them together to make a greater impact, and stitch to the base of the mask.

Do be generous and make lots of 'danglies' to attach. The idea is either to go for a clean-cut image with nothing to spoil the line, or to have lots and really make a splash.

Another material that makes lovely tassels and drops is Shrinking Plastic. This is an unpromising material at first glance, looking like a piece of old plastic but, when coloured with crayons and gold felt-tip pens, it can be heated until it shrinks. It then thickens and the colours become brilliant and stained-glass-like,

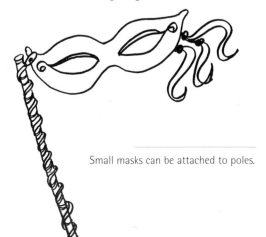

Small masks can be attached to poles.

High-relief embroidery

Several methods can be used to raise the surface of a stitched piece to produce a very high-relief effect, and this can really give impact to what may be a very simple design. This technique is well established in the field of goldwork and metal thread embroidery but can also be used in less gilded pieces, which creates quite a different effect.

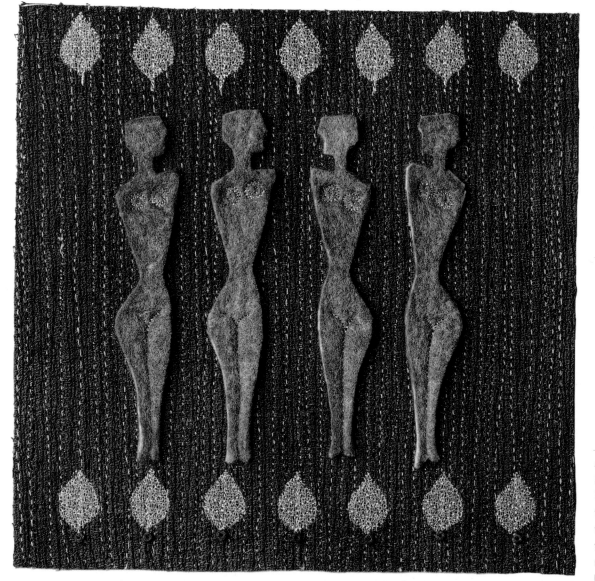

A detail from a large hanging inspired by Ruby Lever's South African travels. The lively figures were cut from thick felt, which were applied to a machine-stitched background.

In Chapter 2, we examined the use of heavy stitch to distort embroidery and make a feature of that distortion. By stitching on a heavier felt and then placing it over more felt, the main lines can be quilted and very raised areas can be created. The design shown here was stitched in massed free running stitch. Heavy stitching to distort the fabric was effective for the wavy lines, which buckled to add interest. Finally the stitched area was cut from the felt and applied to painted silk. The whole thing was laid over more felt and further machining was added to quilt the figures. Water-soluble paper, with Puff Paint, adds a contrast. It is possible to

Above: Design for *Figures in a Landscape*.
Left: *Figures in a Landscape* (Deb Jackson's collection). Heavy machine stitching was placed over felt and quilted using free-machine embroidery. An area of water-soluble paper and Puff Paint adds texture.

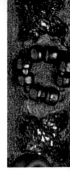

raise the stitching even more with the use of thick padding. Try placing carpet felt or thick heat-moulding foam beneath a fabric and stitching around it to create a really high-relief area. This could mean wrapping the fabric around the cut-out felt first and then applying it, or using the method described below.

1   Cut out the shape in foam or felt. Place it on the prepared background, lay the top fabric over it, and pin each side, keeping a tight tension on the fabric over the shape. A fabric with a little give in it, like stretchy velvet, really helps here.

2   Hand stitch all around the shape using a small back stitch. Get in very close to the shape and keep the fabric firmly stretched over it.

3   When stitching is complete, cut the surrounding fabric away completely.

4   Stitch a cord close to this border, covering the join and raw edge.

On the sample in the photograph bottom right, felt was used for the background fabric and this was zapped with a heat gun when the stitching was finished.

In this design sheet a drawing of acanthus leaves has been interpreted using (top right) Wireform and foam, (bottom left) Wireform and soluble paper, and (bottom right) foam on zapped felt.

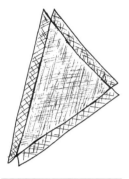

Snipping into the corners of a Wireform shape.

Raised Wireform shapes on a background.

Mountboard frames with stitched pieces attached. The Wireform is securely fastened to the stitched pieces.

Foam and Wireform

It is also possible to use Wireform as a backing for the foam, to create raised surfaces that undulate. You could cover the foam with fabric, as before, or perhaps use it as it is, and texture and paint its surface. In the piece shown on the design sheet on the previous page, I used soft tissues and stitched them to the wire. I then thoroughly wetted it and pushed the wet tissue into crinkles. When dry, I painted them. The leaves were made by dipping the foam shapes into Puff Paint after cutting to shape. When they were dry, I placed a real leaf over the leaf shape and then pressed lightly with a hot iron through parchment paper. The veins of the leaf impressed themselves into the Puff Paint. Use a fresh leaf for each shape or it may stick. The shapes were dabbed with tea to colour them and, when dry, were hand stitched to the Wireform and paper backing. The wire was buckled to distort the shape and throw the foam leaves into greater relief. A gold wax was rubbed lightly over it all afterwards.

You will see from this that the heat-moulding foam has lots of uses. You could also try making leaves using water-soluble paper and Puff Paint. When dissolved, painted and gilded, as described on page 39, they can look quite spectacular.

Using Wireform for raised areas

Here we have yet another use for this wire product. Think about making folded shapes from the wire, which will raise them above a background. Cut a shape from the wire (geometric shapes are probably easiest to begin with) and stitch fabric to it. Allow extra around the edge so it folds under. Embellish with more stitching if you wish. Snip into the corners, as though you were making a mitre. Fold along the lines and cut off the overlaps. Attach to a base fabric by taking the stitching up from the base into the wire as unobtrusively as possible. Alternatively, the shape could be left free-standing

and just be attached at the top or even allowed to hang freely over a background.

An alternative version of this could be to fit the shapes into the central 'empty' area of a frame. It may be worth finding an old frame in a junk shop and using the wooden front as a starting point. Take the shape and size of the inner area and draw suitable shapes to fill it. Given the nature of the product, these should be geometric but could have organic and free-flowing areas as additional embroidery. You will need fairly solid embroidery down two of the opposite sides so that you can stitch the central shapes to them. These side pieces are firmly stapled to a card frame as a solid base. Consider covering and embroidering the wire before folding into shape. Work out how the pieces will join together and then stitch to the edges that are held to the card. Finally decide on the covering for the wooden frame. This could be the plastic canvas method glued to mountboard that has been cut to size (see page 95). Alternatively, the heat-moulding foam could be used, in which case it could be stuck directly to the wood.

Having a frame with no backing allows you to play interesting games with shadows when lighting is directed at the piece. In the piece shown opposite, the work was on the theme of the eternal triangle and words were stitched onto sheer fabric and added to the piece to represent the shadowy figure forming part of the triangle. It can be very interesting working in this way and considering how work is to be mounted at the very beginning of the design process. So often a lot of time is spent in making a beautiful embroidery that is then hastily placed in the first handy frame.

Eternal Triangle
(30 x 26 cm/12 x 10^{1}/$_{4}$ in).
Wireform shapes were sus-
pended in an outer frame.
Having no backing to the
central area allows light to
shine through and project
the lettering onto a wall.

Chapter 6

Three-dimensional Constructions

Next, a very brief look at the truly three-dimensional form – no frames or backgrounds. Many of the materials used throughout the book will lend themselves to constructed textiles. These may take the form of caskets, bowls, vessels, and towers – innovative ways to display your embroideries, held within a three-dimensional frame.

Materials

Most of the materials from the previous chapter are used again here. Heat-moulding foam and Wireform can support the weight of a three-dimensional structure. Thick card can be covered with fabric and the lightweight foam-board is good here as it is light but strong. Plastic canvas is strong and adaptable, and can be stitched to form structures. Ideas for decoration are based on materials and techniques used throughout the book, so this chapter brings them all together in some new, exciting ways.

Constructed displays

Many people do not want to display their work as panels or hangings and it is possible, with a little ingenuity, to devise some alternatives. I call these displays 'mantelpieces' as it is possible to stand them up on a shelf or a windowsill. Windows allow the light to play a part in the effect created but do bear in mind that too much light, especially direct sunlight, can be very bad for textiles. This treatment is best for smaller pieces as larger ones would overbalance. Take care to think of the look of the whole piece when planning the frame shape. The surround could echo the shape of the embroidery or elements could be incorporated that link the two entities together.

Work displayed in this way needs a support of some kind to hold it upright. This can either be a type of plinth to which the stitched piece is attached, or some kind of freestanding frame could be designed to enclose it.

This large-scale work is called *Heavenly Mountains* (122 x 38 cm/48 x 15 in) and was inspired by Russian icons. Maker Sue Cranwell buttonholed the wire frame using wool, silk and cotton threads. The background was created using machine-stitched yarn and fabric with some use of sheers.

Another fossil study using cut-back appliqué for the central motif. French knots were worked within the shapes. It was mounted on a plinth with dowels set into it to support the backing, which is Bondawebbed brown paper over foam.

The plinth could be something fairly simple like a block of wood with lengths of dowel glued to it. This base could be covered with tissue paper and painted, or with pieces of stitched plastic canvas that have been given the tissue-paper treatment. It is then a relatively simple matter to attach cords to the back of an embroidery and tie it to the dowelling posts. This can look attractive if the colour of the cord and the way it is tied or lashed to the posts is well thought through.

Another way to create this three-dimensional effect is to place plastic canvas over strips of thick card, making the canvas slightly longer than the card. Stick the canvas firmly to the card using PVA or contact adhesive. Then cover with tissue and join the lengths together by oversewing the canvas at the narrow edges to form an enclosed shape.

Three strips could form a triangle or you could make a four-sided figure with different-sized pieces. Obviously if the canvas is to be stitched, this should be done before it is glued to the card. Paint the whole thing all over when it is finished. This structure will make a frame for your piece of work, which should be attached to the inside of the frame by stitching it to the underlying string at the joins.

These are just a few ideas but I'm sure that you will think of lots more. Try doing some doodling for ideas for the frame before you even start the embroidery. Working this way round could prove an inspiration (although in general, the frame should be subservient to the embroidery).

Plastic canvas over thick card is formed into a triangular piece.

Of his Bones are Coral Made. This piece was held within an outer frame that was made from a triangle of mountboard covered with stitched plastic canvas. This was lashed to the wooden base with string and the whole thing covered with tissue and painted.

Boxes and caskets

We tend to think of boxes as being very solid but they can be made from craft Vilene (Pellon). This is strong enough to support a lightweight construction, especially if it is used double. This allows some lateral thinking in the design, as much softer effects can be produced.

The well-tried method of making boxes from fabric-covered card can produce some delightful results. Make a plan of the proposed box using light card or heavy paper and try stapling it together to make sure that it works before cutting out of heavier card. Then work the embroidery for each side. Boxes should be carefully thought through so that the embroidery suits the shape of the box. Cut the shapes from thick card and spray with temporary adhesive, then place the embroidery over the top. Lace it on the reverse side by taking a heavy thread from side to side, stitching the long sides first. Follow with the narrow sides and then neaten the corners. Join each piece using a curved needle and ladder stitch.

Initial Vessel by Jeanne Craen (height 25 cm/10 in). Jeanne used letters as a base for the machine stitching. Consideration was given to the shape of the letters to ensure that they fitted the available space. The stitched fabric was then stretched over card and ladder stitch used to join the sides.

Elli Woodsford's *Memory Corset* is a corset-shaped box that contains little bags of memorabilia. Dried flowers, tickets and other precious ephemera are held in the sheer fabric bags.

A selection of vessels. From left to right: A large plastic canvas casket, a coiled pot, a polymer clay tower, and a vessel made from napkin rings and pipe-cleaners.

Boxes can also be made using the card and plastic canvas method. Cut the plastic slightly larger than the card to allow it to be stitched. Then cover with tissue, as before. Do any stitching with string first. Now paint the panels and allow to dry before using strong thread or yarn to join the pieces, first to the base and then to each other, as shown.

The casket shown right has six sides that can be stitched together before being stitched to a base. The lid is made from thick card with panels of plastic canvas applied before being tissued, painted, and waxed.

The base of a hexagonal casket made from plastic canvas. This has been covered with tissue paper and painted. One side has now been stitched to the box.

It is the initial design, followed by attention to the finishing details, that makes all the difference and lifts a simply shaped box into a class of its own. Look at ceramics in museums and books. Some wonderful boxes were made in the 17th century and decorated with raised embroidery techniques. We can learn a lot from sources like these.

Bowls

Bowls can be any shape, from almost flat structures, slightly bent at the edges, to conventional bowl shapes. They need not necessarily be round or particularly deep. Wireform really comes into its own for this sort of shape and is used as a base for all the following ideas.

Make a bowl from separate pieces of fabric-covered Wireform. Join them together at the base and then bend the separate pieces. This technique works best if you cut the pieces from paper or light card and staple them together to work out the shape first.

For flatter bowls, first make a base of Wireform. I prefer to use two layers of the fine wire rather than one of the thicker one for these bases. Cut the wire, cover with base fabric and stitch. Stitch fabric to top and bottom and bend into the required tray shape. Then try one of these methods:

- Make patterns over the base fabric with a glue gun. Colour with paint or wax.

- Use Friendly Plastic, as described in Chapter 5 (page 106), to form a decoration.

- Hand stitch plaits of pipe-cleaners, zapped felt strips, etc. closely over the base.

- Make long strips of zapped felt stuffed with coloured silk, as for the beads. Couch to the base fabric.

- Wrap strips of heat-moulding foam around a pencil. Couch to the base and paint or wax.

Another way of constructing a more conventionally shaped bowl would be to use the coiled pot method, using twists of zapped felt and beaded, wrapped pipe-cleaners.

Twist these together and stitch to make a long length. Coil them around each other, stitching as you go, so that the structure grows upwards. Almost any chunky length or plait works for this, so put on your thinking-cap. I made one by wrapping quite heavy wire with coloured silk and then zapping felt over it. When it was finished it rather resembled a 'slinky' toy (the sort that walks downstairs). However, when I added wrapped pipe-cleaners and beads between the coils, it worked very well.

The pot on the left was made from three wire napkin rings joined using wrapped, beaded pipe-cleaners. Small scraps of machine embroidery have been used in the gaps. The right-hand pot was constructed from a length of wire covered with strips of 'zapped' felt. Wrapped pipe-cleaners and beads were used in coils in the spaces between the wire.

Vessels

As you can imagine, it is possible to use most of the methods described earlier in this chapter and change the shape to make all kinds of vessels. Heat-moulding foam could be cut in petal shapes, heated and moulded over a vase or bowl to produce curves. It could then be joined by using insertion stitches along each edge. I would suggest joining the sides first, then placing the piece over a sheet of paper and drawing around the base. Cut this, slightly smaller, from foam and join using a curved needle.

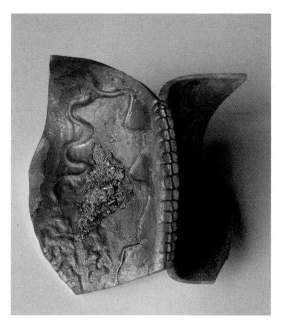

Two sides of a shaped foam vessel have been joined using a strong yarn and buttonhole stitch.

Decorate with stitch and/or impress elements into heated foam. Add found objects, such as shells, by wrapping them tightly with wire and then stitching the wire to the foam. I find that florists' wire is good for this but there are also some lovely enamelled wires in vibrant colours that can be purchased from specialist shops. Keep the stitching neat or paste tissue paper over the inside to cover it. You may find it easier to paint or wax the vessel and stitch on the decoration before sewing up the sides and base. A fun method for vessels is to buy wire shapes and adapt them. Wire napkin rings, Christmas decorations and pot-pourri holders are all good bases. The napkin rings can be joined together with wire and cut-out strips of stitching, or wrapped and beaded pipe-cleaners can be threaded through them. Make a base from painted craft Vilene (Pellon).

How about making vessels from glue? Work on non-stick parchment paper, having made an edge from pipe-cleaners. Use the glue gun over and between the pipe-cleaners – work to a rough design or draw it onto the parchment paper. Make each side separately and stitch, wire, or glue them together afterwards. Use paint or glue to colour the sides before joining.

One side of a vessel is formed using a glue gun on baking paper. A wrapped pipe-cleaner forms a firm outer shape. Metallic wax and tiny beads add lustre to the finish. (MG)

Two towers made from heat-moulding foam impressed with a wooden block. Buttonhole stitch was used to join the sides. The tower on the left is an exuberant sampler of just about everything that can be done to the foam, including adding pieces, laminating with tissue, couching threads, and hand stitching.

Towers

I have a particular fondness for tower structures and, although it could be argued that they are just tall vessels, they need more consideration at the design stage. Think about the shape. Will all the sides be the same shape? Could one, or even two, have sloping sides? Plan the decoration carefully.

The construction materials will need to be fairly strong to support the height, or heavy wires could be used to support the sides if a lightweight material is desired. The wire could be wrapped with yarn or left uncovered if it is a good colour. Heat-moulding foam makes good towers and so does Wireform. Plastic canvas over mountboard also works well.

A tower (height
14 cm/5^1/$_2$ in) made
from polymer clay.
Satay sticks were stuck
in a clay base and
cooked. Tiles of clay
were impressed with a
block, and cords were
pressed into them
before cooking. These
cords were then used
to tie the tiles to the
sticks. Machine-
stitched beads were
used as trimmings.

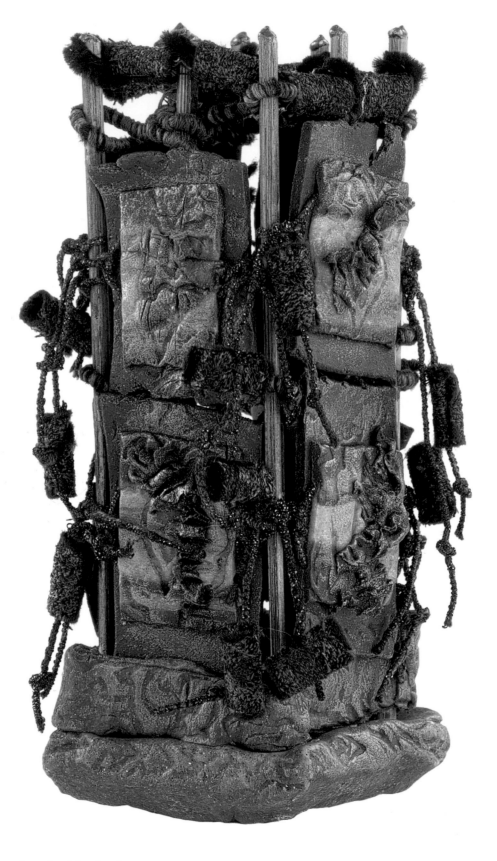

Consider making a polymer clay base with kebab sticks stuck into it. More polymer clay strips could be woven through the sticks. These strips could be textured or impressed with stamps or blocks. They would need to be pressed into the sticks to hold them in position and some thought should be given to keeping the structure to a size that will fit into the oven! It can be made in stages and baked between each stage. For instance, the base and sticks could be baked to give firmness and the clay weavings added before baking again.

Leave room in between the clay to weave through some textile elements when the clay is cool. These could be wired plaits, or strips of automatic pattern or machine embroidery.

Alternatively, bake the clay base with the sticks in and use wrapped pipe-cleaners to hold the sticks in place at the top. Then use clay to form separate flat tiles that could be joined by cords running through holes in the tiles (remember to make the holes before cooking the tiles). The cords could tie the tiles to the kebab sticks forming each side. These sticks could also be wrapped with cords.

The clay base with sticks lends itself to other woven forms, leaving out the clay. Cut out strips of automatic or pulled pattern, stitched on felt. Tie knots in it to make it more substantial. Prepare machine embroidery tiles and cut them out in the same way. Attach the embroidered tiles in the same way as the clay ones.

There are so many ways to construct stitched three-dimensional shapes. Given some starting points, the best way forward is to experiment with shapes, materials, and designs to find your own favourite methods.

Conclusion

I hope this book has given you some ideas for raising the surface of your embroidery. Experiment, and never be afraid to try something new. Keep looking for colour, texture, and shape. Go to museums. Draw and paint. Use this book as a launch pad for your own ideas and, most important of all, enjoy the journey. Have fun!

Resources

Sewing machines

Bernina, Bogod Machine Company, 50–52 Great Sutton Street, London EC1V 0DJ

Brother, Shepley Street, Guide Bridge, Audenshaw, Manchester M34 5JD

Husqvarna/Pfaff, Husqvarna/Viking House, Cheddar Business Park, Wedmore Road, Cheddar, Somerset BS27 3EB

Janome, Janome Centre, Southside, Bredbury, Stockport, Cheshire SK6 2SP

Equipment and materials

The following suppliers have a mail order service and will send you a catalogue.

Art Van Go, The Studios, 1 Stevenage Road, Knebworth, Herts SG3 6AN
email: art@artvango.co.uk
(Angelina, texture mediums, heat-moulding foam [Softsculpt, Formafoam], Wireform, Model Magic, heat tools, respirators, masks, Markal [Shiva] oilsticks, metallic wax, bronze powders, Pearl-Ex, Xpandaprint, Supermend, all art supplies)

Boots the Chemists, multiple outlets
(nappy liners)

June Carroll, 137 Mildmay Road, Chelmsford, Essex CM2 0DT
email: jac@mildmay63.freeserve.co.uk
(Grilon thread)

Franklyn's of Colchester, tel. 01206 563955 or 574758
(Flower Stitcher)

Jennifer Gail Threads, 1–3 Poole Hill, Bournemouth BH2 5PW
email: jenny@jg-threads.freeserve.co.uk
(dyed gimp thread for wrappings, knitting ribbon)

Gillsew, Boundary House, Moor Common, Lane End, Bucks HP14 3HR
email: gillsew@ukonline.co.uk
(Deco-Form, interesting printing blocks, embroidery supplies, Xpandaprint, heat-moulding foam, Tyvek paper)

Ivy House Studio, 37 High Street, Kessingland, Suffolk NR33 7QQ
email: ivyhousestudio@hotmail.com
(Xpandaprint, zappable felt, embossing powders, gizmo tools, water-soluble fabric and paper, embroidery supplies, foils)

Lazertran, 8 Alban Square, Aberaeron, Ceredigion SA46 0LX
email: mic@lazertran.com
(Lazertran transfer paper)

Mulberry Silks, Mulberry Silks, Old Rectory Cottage, Easton Grey, Malmesbury, Wilts SN16 0PE
email: patricia.wood@rdplus.net
(vibrant silk threads for wrapping pipe-cleaners)

Oliver Twists, 22 Phoenix Road, Crowther, Washington, Tyne & Wear NE38 0AD
email: jean@olivertwists.freeserve.co.uk.
(enamelled wire, threads, especially thicker threads for wrapping and cable stitch)

Rainbow Silks, 6 Wheelers Yard, High Street, Great Missenden, Buckinghamshire HP16 0AL
email: rainbowsilks@rainbowsilks.co.uk
(Angelina, metallic paints, embossing powders, heat-moulding foam [Softsculpt, Formafoam], Wireform, Markal [Shiva] oilsticks, metallic wax,

bronze powders, Friendly Plastic, Shrinking Plastic, Impress Me stamps)

Stitch 'n' Craft, Swan's Yard Craft Centre, High Street, Shaftesbury, Dorset SP7 8JQ
email: enquiries@stitchncraft.co.uk
(Gizmo tool, beads)

Strata, Oronsay, Misbourne Avenue, Chalfont St Peter, Bucks SL9 0PF
email: gwen@ghed.freeserve.co.uk
(chiffon scarves, Xpandaprint, heat-moulding foam, Tyvek paper, Fibretex)

Winifred Cottage, 17 Elms Road, Fleet, Hampshire GU13 9EG
email: WinifCott@aol.com
(chiffon scarves, threads [including YLI Fusible], silk and viscose tops)

Liz Welch, 61 Shelford Road, Radcliffe-on-Trent, Notts NG12 1HA
email: lizzie@dial.pipex.com

Artstraws, plastic canvas, and polymer clay are all available from art or hobby shops, and glue guns from hardware stores. Bondaweb (fusible webbing) is available from haberdashers

North America
Most materials in this book are available from art shops, but specifically:

Embroidery Adventures
email: reliker@embroideryadventures.com

Gerber EZ-Liner Diaper Liners, 800-4-GERBER
(diaper liners)

Impress Me, www.impressmenow.com
(Impress Me stamps)

Kunin Felt, 380 Lafayette Road, Hampton, NH 03842, USA
tel: 800-292-7900
(zappable felt)

Meinke Toys, PMB#411, 55 E Long Lake Rd, Troy MI 48085, USA
tel: 248-813-9806, fax. 801-991-5983
email: meinketoy@mindspring.com
(most supplies)

Nancy's Notions, www.nancysnotions.com
(Flower Stitcher)

Australia and New Zealand
The Thread Studio, 6 Smith Street, Perth 6000, Western Australia
tel: +61 (0)9 227 1561,
email: dale@thethreadstudio.com
(most supplies)

New Zealand
Craft Supplies, 31 Gurney Road, Belmont, Lower Hutt, New Zealand
(most supplies)

Books

A basic knowledge of machine embroidery has been assumed for this book. To learn machine embroidery, I recommend *The Machine Embroidery Workbook* (ISBN 0 903562 27 8) by Valerie Campbell-Harding and Maggie Grey, published in the UK by the Embroiderers' Guild, www.embroiderersguild.com
Also, *Machine Embroidery Stitch Techniques* (ISBN 0 7134 5797 X) by Valerie Campbell-Harding and Pamela Watts published by Batsford.

Index